How To Write Slices of Life

The Episode Approach to Memoir Writing

by

Edmund Hansen

authorHOUSE™

1663 LIBERTY DRIVE, SUITE 200
BLOOMINGTON, INDIANA 47403
(800) 839-8640
WWW.AUTHORHOUSE.COM

First published by AuthorHouse 06/15/05

ISBN: 1-4208-4129-7 (sc)

Printed in the United States of America
Bloomington, Indiana

This book is printed on acid-free paper.

Other books by the author:
(1)   A Father's Story: The Story of a Son's Battle with AIDS.
(2)   From Grandson to Grandfather: Reflections of a University Professor on his Career and Family.
(3)   Grin And Share It: The story of a loyal daughter's quest for a meaningful relationship with her mother.

DEDICATION

This book is dedicated to **Frank P. Thomas**, a memoir writing teacher par excellent.

Frank moved to Sun City Center in 1979. Seeing a need for helping residents write their memoirs he began teaching a memoir writing course. Some of the places he taught this course were The Ruskin Library, Prince of Peace Catholic Church, Eckerd College Elderhostel and United Community Church Community College.

In 1984 Frank wrote the book <u>How to Write The Story of Your Life</u>. Writer's Digest Books of Cincinnati, Ohio published the book (ISBN 0-89879-359-9). Frank always viewed this accomplished with much satisfaction. To this day his book is considered the 'bible' of memoir writing. I had Frank as a teacher in 1999 and considered him a friend.

After teaching memoir writing for 21 years ill health forced him to step aside. He passed away April 6, 2004 and will be sorely missed.

From me and the many thousands of your students -- 'thanks' for your contribution to our writing of our memoirs.

INTRODUCTION

The first memoir that I read was written in 1981 by Carl W. Danhouser, my Uncle Carl. Carl died in 1994 at the age of 91.

What a treasure trove of family history. Carl, born Carl Wilhelm Heinrich Damsheuser, relates in chapter one about kerosene lamps (no electricity), a wood burning stove in the kitchen, a wood shed with an attached three holer --- one smaller hole for the children --- and cleaning father's spittoon.

His memoirs are 98 double-spaced typewritten pages with seven pages of pictures. A copy machine was used for making copies including the pictures.

Of all the books in my library this is the one I would grab in the event of fire. It is that valuable to me.

This is what you will start in this class: writing your memories for your relatives, and they will cherish them as much as I cherish Uncle Carl's.

TABLE OF CONTENTS

CHAPTER ONE
MEMOIR WRITING

.... astonished at mankind's.... attempts.... to leave our mark in the unset concrete of time – something to say we existed.... If we write but one book in life, let it be our autobiography.

Prologue to Timepiece
Richard Paul Evans

<u>What is a memoir?</u>

A memoir is a work of non-fiction based on personal experience; in this situation, your experience. A memoir differs from an autobiography in that the former is the pouring out of your collective memories as best you remember them. An autobiography requires the writer to do as much research as possible in order to relate the facts as accurately as possible. The memoirist relates what he remembers and how he felt at the time of the experience. It is not that you don't want facts correct but that the autobiographer has a greater degree of obligation for research.

The written memoir links generations and provides a personal history for succeeding generations. It is our 'footprints' showing where we went. Like the etching of initials by a child in soft cement our story is a reminder that we exist, lived and loved leaving this heritage for others.

Why do we write memoirs?

Probably the most important reason for writing memoirs is the lasting legacy aspect for those following behind us in the family chain. It is a priceless gift; for any other gift they have MasterCard. But only you can give this gift.

It is important for you to know that as you reflect back on life's experiences that as humans we relive these experiences. The same emotions that were experienced originally will return. But you will now experience them with decades of living to draw upon and perhaps, just perhaps, you will modify that memory. Either way expect some emotional involvement on your part and receive the therapeutic value from reviewing past important moments.

What should go into a memoir?

Certainly it is important to write about life's highlights and significant events. Your dating, marriage and birth of each child are a story by itself. Remembrances of your parents and how life was lived in the "old days" will be appreciated by the younger generations.

Life's adversities are very important to share because character is hewed out of adversity. Tribulation is the test tube from which man is refined and impurities removed.

How you loved; your desires; your longings, these will expose what you share with humanity.

All people have experienced turning points. Those forks-in-the-road we took and mentors encountered either determined or gave direction to our walk in life.

We will spend a lot more time on the above items in the course of the next six weeks.

Edmund Hansen

<u>Why do we read other people's memoirs?</u>

Reading the memoirs of others give us a chance to reflect upon the similarities of our shared human existence and the differences, which identify our uniqueness. Our own remembrances come flooding back during this reading thus serving us as "memory sparklers", a chance to revisit our past.

Our culture places the rich and famous on a pedestal so a glut of celebrity memories is available. Some of these are politically motivated but others are very good and remind us that most of these people were once commoners like us.

What is a partial memoir?

A partial memoir is one written on only a portion of one's life. Commercially available memoirs, which are partial memoirs, include:

Hour Before Daylight by Jimmy Carter (first 20 years of life).

Angela's Ashes by Frank McCourt (first 18 years of life).

'Tis by Frank McCourt (takes over after Angela's Ashes).

A common partial memoir by men is to write about their war experiences. Those in professional sports tend to write on their career.

Do you remember when?

Wood burning stoves were used instead of electric or gas?

An actual ice box kept food cold instead of a refrigerator?

A *25* or *50* sign was placed in the window to communicate to the ice man the size chunk of ice needed?

Ice was sawed from lakes and stored in ice houses for summer use?

Throw rugs were used before the invention of wall-to-wall carpeting?

Taking throw rugs outdoors for cleaning was done by placing them over the clothesline and beating the tarnation out of them (before vacuum cleaners)?

Everyone had an outhouse instead of toilets to take care of mother nature. And chamber pots for night hour use?

Clothes were hung on a clothesline to dry?

Homes didn't have heating ducts but holes covered by grates for the purpose of heating upstairs bedrooms by gravity (hot air rises)?

No air conditioning, TV or bottled beer?

Children were quarantined when they got measles or mumps?

The Omar man brought baked goods?

Milk in glass bottles was delivered by a man with a horse drawn wagon?

Grandparents lived with their children and sometimes moving periodically between the children?

Movies would show a newsreel before the main feature so we would have a visual image of current events? Perhaps we did have a cartoon also.

There wasn't fast food except peanut butter on bread?

No one knew about credit cards, acid-washed Levi's, ATMs or cell phones?

Everyone sat and ate supper together?

Spam was something you ate instead of delete?

Depression was an economic condition instead of either a precursor to a storm or a state of the mind?

The story you will tell is how life was lived in the 'ole days' in spite of no TV, DVDs, body piercing, underarm deodorant, cell phones, your own car at age 16 paid for by daddy, or rave dances. Do it now. Time marches on. Your grandchildren want to know you better.

CHAPTER TWO
MY STRENGTH IS STORY TELLING

Memory is the crux of our humanity. Without memory we have no identity. That is really why I am committing an autobiography.

Erica Jong (1942 --)

How will this course help you?

Having written my memoirs I have some very definite ideas about what worked for me and what didn't. What I intend to do is tell you what I did, why I did it and how I did it. Then I will place this in a broader context by including ideas other authors used. All of this is to be viewed by you as a mammoth buffet of information and ideas. You then make your selection from all that is available.

There isn't a 'right way' and a 'wrong way'. It's selecting what you think will work for you.

Then we will have you start writing and several will have the chance to read what they wrote to the class. It is not the purpose of reading to have the class become your judge and critic. You will do that for yourself having read other author's memoirs, upon hearing what others in class have written and seeing your writing improve during the course of the class.

Will the instructor read and critique your work?

That's a yes and a no. I do expect everyone to hand in what has been written for each class and I enjoy reading non-fiction writing, including yours. Critiquing is another issue.

All of you will have someone – maybe yourself – type what is written on a computer. This includes an editing, as the computer will correct spelling, adjust what is written for correct grammar and make suggestions for the use of commas, colons and semi-colons.

This is not an English writing class where the purpose is to improve writing. It's a written story telling class and the purpose is to be able to transfer a story from your head to that of another through the written word. Precise use of written English be damned. Memoir writing is the Folk Art of Writing. Whatever we do is correct.

This attitude doesn't mean that you shouldn't conform your writing to the generally accepted norms of writing. It does mean not to get all hung up on techniques to the point that you give up and do nothing. Written English grows and changes and what is today, like women's clothing fashions, may not be in tomorrow.

I often tell the story about a Christmas card I received one Christmas. It was from a cousin I had recently renewed my acquaintance with. The letter had no words capitalized, no periods and no commas. While it took me three or four readings before I could mentally adjust to his style I was very pleased for his note. I would rather have this type of communication then one from a cousin with perfect grammar who never wrote.

Our class will contain individuals who are writers or English teachers and those who haven't written anything but a check for the last fifty years. Your relatives will appreciate whatever is written.

With the divergence of writing experience and ability it is very important that you do not compare yourself with your classmates or with me. Folk Art Writing, like Folk Art, is the writing of the masses and is an entity unto itself.

CHAPTER THREE
YOUR LIFE AS A COMPOSITE
OF SHORT STORIES

To write well, express yourself like the common people, but think like a wise man.

Aristotle (384 - 322 B.C.)

A new neighbor moves in next door to you. As a welcoming gesture you invite them over for a beverage. The conversation starts with: where are you from?; how many children do you have?; what was your profession, career or job?; are you snowbirds?

As you become better acquainted the stories unique to you begin to be told. Such stories as not making it to the hospital for your second child's birth and delivering in the car, or when you won a special event. These stories are about an event, occurrence or memorable situation.

When writing memoirs you are writing – not telling – these special stories. All of them. That is, all the stories that define the life you lived.

Writing a memoir seems somewhat daunting at first thought. Yet it can be broken down into bite size pieces. The old cliché works here, how does one eat an elephant? One bite at a time. In short, a task will not be overwhelming if you can reduce it to its smallest component.

We will call these "bite size pieces" – episodes. An episode is a slice of your life; a self-contained short story. Roughly 100 short stories will communicate to your children and grandchildren what life, for you, was all about.

Much of our time in this course will be spent on selecting these 100 stories, how best to write them, how to add color and to actually get started. Time will be spent on the overall organization to use for memoir writing.

All right gang. Let's get going.

CHAPTER FOUR
STEP ONE IN GETTING STARTED IS TO SEQUENCE A LIFE CHRONOLOGY

Plan ahead. It wasn't raining when Noah built the ark.

Unknown

The very first step is to write down and date as many of the key events in your life as possible. I found myself using 4 by 6 inch index cards. Just get it down then arrange the cards chronologically. If you are a computer person just translate this into computerize.

This is something you can work on for two or three weeks. As you can see from my chronology I use bullet statements instead of complete sentences. My purpose was to display my life in front of me to identify my life's stages. Many people include their chronology in the appendix of the memoir book for a quick glimpse of their life. If you do this perhaps complete sentences is more appropriate.

Remember the purpose of this exercise is to have your key events before you for the purpose of identifying your life's stages.

MY LIFE CHRONOLOGY

1936	Born March 9th at St. Elizabeth Hospital in Appleton, WI
1941	Moved to the house I would live in until college
1941	Started kindergarten
1941-1946	Grandpa lived with us
1941-1945	WWII
1946	Grandpa died
1948-1951	Junior high school
1948-1952	Paper route
1952	Started dating
1952-1954	Worked at the Appleton Post Crescent Formed a 'group' with Hugh, Jim and Tom
1951-1954	High school
1954	Met Ginny
>>>	
1954-1956	First two years of college
1956	Married Our first home
1956-1958	Last two years of college
>>>	
1958	First son born 7/24/58 Moved to Wausau, WI for first teaching job

1959-1960	Attended academic year and following summer session at University of Kansas Second son born 10/24/59
1960-1963	Moved to Manitowoc, WI for second teaching job Attended Tulane University the summers of 1961 and '62
>>>	
1963-1965	Moved to Oshkosh, WI to teach at University of Wisconsin Third son born 12/25/63
1964	Purchased the house we would live in for 23 years Attended summer session at University of Kansas Summer 1964
1965-1966	Attended academic year at University of Kansas
1966-1994	Taught at University of Wisconsin
1967	Fourth son born 1/7/67
1974-1985	Sons participated in high school sports
1970-1982	Sons had paper route
1970	Father to nursing home
1972-1977	Camping
>>>	
1977	First son's high school graduation
1978	Second son's high school graduation
1977-1980	First son in Army
1978	Father died
1979	Mother in nursing home and we sponsor refugees

1982	Third son's high school graduation
	Second son's marriage
	Third son moves to Colombia, South America for ½ year

1983   First and second sons' college graduations and first son's marriage

1985   Fourth son's high school graduation

1985   Problem with third son

1986   Family homestead sold – moved to condo

>>>

1987   Fourth son's marriage
Third son's college graduation and moves to Phoenix

1987, 1989, 1990, 1991, 1994
Birth of grandchildren

1991   Third son seriously ill

1992   Fourth son's college graduation

1993   Third son died
First son critically wounded in Somalia
I became ill

>>>

1994   I'm forced to retire, physically disabled
We move to Florida

1995   Mother died

1995-1999   Cruises, Elderhostels, trips to Wisconsin and Florida activities

CHAPTER FIVE
STEP TWO IS IDENTIFYING
YOUR LIFE STAGES

For books are more than books. They are the life, the very heart and core of ages past, the reason why men lived and worked and died, the essence and quintessence of their lives.

Amy Lowell (1874 – 1925)

The second step is to analyze your life chronology looking for natural breaks; those demarcation points where you clearly entered another stage.

For me it seemed initially to be my living arrangement, which set things apart. Leaving my family of origin for college in 1954 represented a definite growth step. My second major growth step was moving 100 miles away from my parents for my first full time job. This occurred in 1958.

Now I was independent of my parents with my own family so separation points involved my relationship with them instead of my parents. Family Living Part II started as my sons began leaving the family thus shrinking our family.

Finally the empty nest and retirement stages came.

Now it's your turn to identify your life stages.

MY STAGES FROM LIFE CHRONOLOGY

Living with my family of origin   1936-1954
(18 years)

College, living separate from family of origin   1954-1958
       And marriage (forming our own family) (4 years)

Transition living dictated by career & births of two sons 1958-1963
       Early full time jobs   (5 years)
       Two sons born
       Seven times we relocated the family

Family living Part I   1963-1975
       Two more sons born   (12 years)
       Living with four sons prior to high school and graduation
       First child born in 1958 and the last to graduate from college
          was in 1992
       Completing my post-graduate education

Family living Part II   1975-1987
       4 high school graduations   (12 years)
        /career choices
     Launching children 3 college graduations
                 3 marriages

Empty nest living and grandchildren   1987-1994
       Boomerang children   (7 years)
       Developing the extended family

Retirement   1994 - on
       Living separate from the extended family

CHAPTER SIX
STEP THREE IS TO FOCUS ON WHAT YOU WANT TO STRESS AND THE NEED TO PRIORITIZE

I never think at all when I write. Nobody can do two things at the same time and do them both well.

Don Marquis (1878 – 1937)

Something discovered very early in memoir writing is the realization that you can't write about everything that happened in a person's lifetime. Things will have to be eliminated. This is the need to prioritize. Just what is it that you want read by others? Not everything that happened to you is of equal importance. What slices of life are truly representative of your life? And what family stories do you want to preserve?

As I pondered this for myself a decision was made to split my memoirs into the family man and the career man. Men of my generation lived two separate lives. Any memoir of me would be incomplete if my career and its' achievements plus trials and tribulations were not included. A working phase may or may not be something you want in your memoirs.

For the family man I wanted to stress family living and my personal and educational development. In the personal development area I wanted to stress: who influenced me, my friendships and my growth in the civil rights area.

In my thirty-five year career in education, especially the thirty-one at the university level, I wanted to explain to my sons about my career path. The vast majority of these years were not spent as a full-time teacher. Instead they were spent on various projects or in administration. I really had a varied career much of which they were unaware. They simply knew I taught at the university.

Once I realized what I wanted to focus on then identifying the one hundred short stories became much easier.

CHAPTER SEVEN
STEP FOUR IS THE MATRIX OF EPISODES AND THE PARTITIONING OF THE STORIES WITHIN STAGES INTO CHAPTERS

We write to taste life twice, in the moment, and in retrospection.... We write to be able to transcend our life, to reach beyond it. We write to teach ourselves to speak with others, to record the journey into the labyrinth.

Anais Nin (1903 – 1977)

It becomes important to be able to display everything in front of you. To do this take a 20 by 30 inch sketch sheet (any art supply store has sketch pads this size) and make an array with stages across the top and focus areas for the left hand column. In my case this makes a four by seven array with a matrix having twenty-eight entries.

Now comes the job of filling in the boxes not all of which will be used. For instance, my career did not occur until stage three. Thus the first two boxes for each career-focused area would be empty.

Certainly your life chronology would provide many entries in your matrix. Keep a small notebook with you at all times and make entries whenever something hits you that you wish to write about. Don't trust your memory to keep this kind of clutter available when you arrive home. Since I have now told you this several times already please conclude that the notebook is very important.

After two or three weeks it will become necessary to repackage all the matrix entries into chapters. Certainly you may use one stage per chapter but I choose not to do this. There just seemed to be natural groupings of like-minded stories that should stand alone as a chapter.

The following is a list of my chapters and the substance of that chapter.

Chapter	Substance of the Chapter
1	Growing Up (age 0 – 15)
2	Teenage Years (ages 15 – 18)
3	First years out of high school (ages 18 – 22)
4	First full-time job & starting a family (ages 22-27)
5	Starting Career (ages 27 – 29)
10	Settling down – raising the family (ages 30 – 41)
14	Launching children (ages 39 – 51)
15	Adjusting to the 'empty nest' (age 50)
18	Boomerang children & grandchildren (ages 51-58)
20	Physically disabled and adjusting to retirement (ages 58 – 62)
21	The retired life (ages 62 on)

THE MATRIX --- ESTABLISHING EPISODES

THE MATRIX --- ESTABLISHING EPISODES

FOCUSED AREAS   *LIFE STAGES*

Focused Areas	1	2	3	4	5	6	7

FAMILY LIVING
My family of origin
Our nuclear family
The extended family
  Grandchildren and
  the Asian side of
  the family							

PERSONAL AND EDUCATION DEVELOPMENT Who influenced me? Friendships and relationships Growth on Black issue Personal growth My education (from Elementary to Grad. School)							

CAREER
Teaching
  The joys and struggles
  with students
Frustrations with bureaucracy
Advisement
Non-advisement and
  Non-teaching							

CAREER PATH DECISIONS Changing jobs--why? What were factors to consider in my career progression? Key documents What did I do in my job?							

CHAPTER EIGHT
STEP FIVE IS TO TRANSFER CHAPTER MATERIAL TO SEPARATE SHEETS WITH ONE SHEET PER CHAPTER

Don't tell me the moon is shining; show me the glint of light on the broken glass.

Anton Chekhov (1860 – 1904)

This chapter re-packaging should be done by transferring the bullets for stories you intend to write for a particular chapter onto a separate sheet of paper. Then place all these sheets in a loose-leaf binder. As you write your short stories they may now be filed into the binder by chapter.

After this re-packaging is completed the matrix is of no more use. Any additional stories you think of may be added directly to your chapter page. As you complete stories a 'tick' mark on the chapter page will remind you that this story is written.

CHAPTER NINE
WRITING POINTERS

If you are in difficulties with a book, try the element of surprise: attack it at an hour when it isn't expecting it.

H. G. Wells (1866 – 1946)

1. Write one episode at a time and they may be written in any order you want.

2. Chose a place to write and keep your materials ready. This is to include such things as a favorite pencil or pen. You want to be able to sit down and write without having to clean up someone else's mess or even to have to evict them from your area. If everything is not convenient the job will not get done.

3. Chose the time of day that best suits you. Some of us are morning people while others of us function best at night.

4. Set aside regular times each week to write. This may be four hours three days a week or some other regular arrangement. If writing your memoirs is the goal than re-arrange your commitments accordingly. What I'm saying is, you cannot add memoir writing to a busy schedule without deleting or postponing something.

5. Either you tell time how it will be spent or it will tell you where it went. Remember that memoir writing is a marathon race and requires pacing. Like running it means frequent sessions on a regular basis.

6. Don't wait for inspiration. Writing is 10% inspiration and 90% perspiration. Writing is like any other hobby. It demands time and with time the passion for writing will come.

7. Don't be overcome by mechanics. Simply write and correct spelling and grammar later; after you're done with the current train of thought. If you're computerized you have built in assistance.

8. A rough draft is always done first. I use skinny lined paper and write on every other line. This permits the liberal use of 'carrots' and erasing. I re-copy at a later time after it has had time to 'jell', be corrected and edited by me. I said 'by me' because you should edit yourself before hiring someone else.

9. Read other autobiographies and memoirs for additional memory sparklers. This will also help you improve your writing and give additional ideas for arranging items in your book.

10. Use simple words. Write like you talk so the reader can envision you telling the story. DO NOT use a thesaurus only to impress the reader with big words. Capture your writing style in such a way that the reader says, "Yes, that sounds just like Aunt Mabel." Memoir writing is the 'folk art' of writing.

11. Writing skills are learned through practice just like learning how to play baseball or driving a car. Practice is what permits you to hone your writing skills. You may even want to re-write earlier written episodes when finished.

12. One can learn to write at any age. It is not a God-given talent that one is born with.

13. Tell your story like you are talking to a friend. You may even want to use a tape recorder and then transcribe the spoken word. Make liberal use of the word 'I'. After the story is completed go back making complete sentences. Then polish the sentences.

14. Avoid rambling. Stephen King, the famous mystery writer, asserts that he deletes 10 percent of his written words when he edits. Always ask yourself if a particular sentence contributes to the story.

15. Get your feelings into your writing. How did something affect you?

16. Keep a small notebook on your person at all times. Capture enough of a thought so that you are able to write the details later.

17. Each episode is to be a unit that can stand alone by itself as a short story. So each episode is to contain all the pertinent information including dates. But not everything has to be in episode format. Chapter 17C starting on page 282 is the best example of this. This chapter was written as narrative and then I added captions to keep the format the same.

18. Link your life to events happening in history. Work in historical occurrences like the depression or when social security was passed.

19. Avoid overloading sentences. Keep them short or run the risk of losing the reader.

20. What, why, when, where, who and how is a journalistic cornerstone. But it is also true in memoir writing. It provides all the information and answers everyone's questions.

21. Re-read and edit after about ten days. This way you will not re-read the same error into your writing. Give your writing time to 'cook'. Re-write if it doesn't sound just right. Hemingway wrote the final paragraph for "For Whom The Bell Tolls" thirty times before he was happy with it.

22. Skip a difficult part and go on. Come back to it later when you are fresh. Remember, using the episode method any episode may be written before another.

23. Get people into your life story. Recognize the people who meant a great deal to you. Refer to the section where I talk about Dr. Phil's five pivotal people in chapter 19.

24. Periodically go back and clean up phrases and make complete sentences. All of us think faster then we can write so go back and clean things up.

25. Sometimes reading a sentence aloud will help. Other times writing again from a different perspective helps.

26.   If you ask someone to edit your work make sure it is your final draft. Pick an objective reader – not a relative – someone who will be honest and frank.

27.   Limit travel talk. Don't bore the reader with a day-by-day account of a vacation. Consider what were the highlights. A daily journal for you to relive a great trip is fine. But don't include it in your memoirs. The same principle holds true when inviting guests to your home. Showing them 20 representative pictures is fine but 200 is not fine.

28.   Limit the use of commas and exclamation marks. Limit underscoring words or a word with all capitals. Instead achieve the emphasis you want by the choice of words.

29.   Keep your writing moving. We all know how boring it is when people speak needlessly slow, include endless meaningless detail or ramble – never making reasonable progress towards the point of the story. Watch out that the same doesn't occur in your writing. Also watch for repetition of words within close proximately of each other. Delete redundancies and needless words or complete sentences that don't contribute to the story.

30.   Spread out your copy. Spread out your pages on a long desk or ironing board. This helps to see if you strayed from the topic, whether paragraphs are too long or if you have introduced repetition. As was stressed earlier, don't ramble or start each sentence with the same word.

31.   Be aware that dialogue slows down the narrative but is worth the investment if used appropriately.

32.   Explain the terms of your generation since seceding generations would not understand the meaning. Examples: lamplighters, the New Deal, corsets, the Tin Lizzie, or crystal sets. My generation talked about an extravagant or top-of-the-line items as the 'cadillac' of that item. My uncle used the word 'doosy' for the same thing. While the Cadillac car was my extravagant car the Duesenberg was my uncle's. See chapter 18 for more on this.

33. Do not copy someone else's style. What you write, your choice of words, how you arrange them, will reflect your own personality and your own way of thinking. Communicate, don't try to impress.

34. Be careful not to use discriminatory pronouns, such as "he" or "his", when referring to both genders. One easy way around this is to use the plural form of "they" or "their". When dealing with work titles, there are many options:

"policeman"	is	"police officer"
" mailman"	becomes	"letter carrier"
"salesman"	becomes	"salesperson"
"fireman"	becomes	"fire fighter"
"stewardess"	becomes	"flight attendant"
"waiter and waitress"	becomes	"server"

35. The three indispensable pages are:

    Title page (one whole page)
    Table of Contents
    Introduction or Forward
        why you wrote the book
        heritage
        reveal yourself
        a treasure more then china, jewelry, money
    Dedication (this is optional)

36. Use of numbers:

    a. Spell out 1 through 10 and use numerals for 11 on
    b. Use numbers of dates: December 7, 1941
    c. Do not start a sentence with a number
    d. Use Arabic numbers for page numbering and locate center and bottom of each page. Start the numbering with the title page.
    e. Use numbers for time: 7 A.M.; 11 P.M.
    f. Be uniform within a sentence.

Edmund Hansen

What Day of the Week?

Formula				Example
	Ancestral wedding date			9 December 1824
Step 1.	Begin with the last 2 digits of the year.			24
Step 2.	Add ¼ of this number and disregard any remainder.			6
Step 3.	Add the date in the month.			9
Step 4.	Add according to the month:			6
	January	1	(for leap year, 0)	
	February	4	(for leap year, 3)	
	March	4		
	April	0		
	May	2		
	June	5		
	July	0		
	August	3		
	September	6		
	October	1		
	November	4		
	December	6		
Step 5.	Add for the century:			2
	18th century	4		
	19th century	2		
	20th century	0		
	21st century	6		
Step 6.	Total the numbers from steps 1–5.			47
Step 7.	Divide by 7. Check the remainder against this chart to find the day of the week:			6 with a remainder of 5. The wedding took place on a Thursday.
	1 = Sunday			
	2 = Monday			
	3 = Tuesday			
	4 = Wednesday			
	5 = Thursday			
	6 = Friday			
	0 = Saturday			

CHAPTER TEN
MULLING THINGS OVER AND WRITING IN THAT LITTLE BOOK. USE OF A TAPE RECORDER. TESTIMONIALS.

The difference between the almost – right word and the right word is really a large matter --- it's the difference between the lightning bug and the lightning.

Mark Twain

Many people after reading my memoirs say, "How did you remember all that?" Folks, once you get started those memories will come flooding back. And they will flood back at the strangest times.

You may be shopping at Publix purchasing broccoli and suddenly after seeing the GREEN broccoli your thoughts go back in time to the summers worked at the local canning factory and green beans. Jot this down – enough to remind you when home. Keep a small notebook on you at all times. If you don't make a note of that fleeting thought it will leave as fast as it came leaving you frustrated trying to think back to it.

Frank Thomas called this notebook your 'constant companion'. He is right. Organize yourself so that these thoughts are retained. I repeat again – keep the notebook on you at all times.

Rest assured that reflecting upon your life lived you will find your memories; they are all there. The job you will eventually have is selecting the best, the most representative, the most life-changing events to include in your memoirs.

We think faster then we write or type. Some have found it helpful to speak into a tape recorder and then transcribe the tape. This is especially helpful when interviewing a relative. By taping the conversation precious time isn't wasted taking notes which breaks the continuity of the relative who is talking.

My suggestion for taping an interview -- that you make a written list of questions before the interview starts. This keeps you in control of the interview, makes sure everything you wanted is asked and keeps everyone on the purpose of the interview. Free wheeling jam sessions just won't cut it.

One can be 'force fed' to help in remembering memories. These are called 'memory sparklers'. A set of memory sparklers is included in chapter 19 with the assignment. But simply reading another person's memoirs will remind you of things you will want to include in your memoirs. Be sure to make a note in your notebook. Don't trust your mind to keep track of this.

I have included two letters I received from relatives after I sent copies of my memoirs. The first, from John Hansen who is a cousin, writes, "your book brings back memories --- beautiful memories of the past I probably would have never again revived and enjoyed if it hadn't been for your beautiful book". Folks, reading memoirs will do this – function as memory sparklers. The second letter was written by a niece. I haven't seen her since 1981. She grew up in California and now lives in Boston. We started exchanging letters in 1993. This is why she writes, "I feel like I know you so much better now." Memoirs will do that.

The last testimonial is a professional review by Writer's Digest.

September 5, 2001

Dear Ed,

Thank you, thank you so very much for sending me "From Grandson To Grandfather." I haven't read it from cover to cover as yet. It seems all I want to do is just thumb my way along reading something here, then something there, always getting impatient and eager to quickly find more Hansen history.

Your book brings back memories-beautiful memories of the past I probably would have never again revived and enjoyed if it hadn't been for your beautiful book. We were richly blessed, being born into a family like the Hansen's. Such shining examples we had to guide us: Grandma, your folks, our aunts and uncles, cousins, the family reunions at Pierces Park and at Uncle Otto and Aunt Kit's cottage on Waverly Beach and last, but not least you and your family. I appreciate your comments regarding my brother Wally and I.

Glad you quit smoking! Ha, I guess we all were guilty of such smoking ventures when young. I, however, went above and beyond mere tobacco branching out to include corn silk rolled in writing paper and coffee grounds smoked in a pipe. I can't believe I did that. Ouch!

Somehow, someway, your "Father's Philosophy" got installed in my brothers Wally, Bob and me. It seems without having been taught these fifteen principles, we knew them and practiced them. I'm thinking we must have just absorbed these virtues via the examples our family constantly set before us in their daily lives.

I'm not certain you fully appreciate how much I'm enjoying your book. I only wish everyone would read your story. Its such a fine example of how our society ought to be. Thanks! Keep on writing Ed!

Our love to you both,

John

9/9/01

Dear Uncle Ed,

Thank you so much for sending your wonderful new book to me! I've had a delightful time reading it. I feel like I know you so much better now. Your sons and grandchildren must be thrilled. Writing that book was a very thoughtful thing to do. I will treasure it always.

My brother, Brian, is fascinated by family history. He's also intrigued when I tell him about you and your writing. He, like me, has often felt disconnected from the family and longs for a more complete sense of belonging. If there is any way you could send him a copy of your book and maybe also the book about Dean, I know he would appreciate it a great deal. His address is, as

Writer's
Digest

2001 Self Published Book Awards
Evaluation Sheet

Title: **From Grandson to Grandfather**
Category: **Life Stories**
Name: **Edmund Hansen**
Address: **1011 Norfork Island Ct.**
City: **Sun City Center**   State: **FL**   Zip: **33573**

What impressed you most about this book?

This is an invaluable document for you and your family — such a treasure. In your introduction, you state that ~~this was your~~ main purpose in writing this book was twofold — for yourself as much as for others. But I think your family will truly find this book a special gift and a lasting one.

I felt that this book did a good job of providing a "slice of life", particular of the life of a young married couple struggling to balance work, family, and each other. I loved the photos — they were well placed and really added to the narrative. Good use of heading to organize the information.

If this were your book what would you do to market it?

This is such a personal story that obviously the first choice would be your friends and family. I'd also suggest that you check out opportunities in the areas in which the story takes place — Appleton, the Universities, Oshkosh, etc. Especially if you still have acquaintances in these places. Perhaps bookstores might want "local" author in for a signing! Also, look into Wisconsin Presses — university; small presses often look for stories set (mostly) in their locale.

I was really moved by your story. There's something touching and wonderful about the accumulation of thoughts and feelings and actions that combine to create a life. I really was affected by your discussion of your son Dean's struggle eventual succumbing to AIDS, your tale of taking in Laotian immigrants, your struggles and joys w/ family, kids.
It's been a great life so far for you, it seems. Thank you for sharing it w/ me, and with the world. I'm sure your friends, family will always treasure this.

CHAPTER ELEVEN
OTHER ORGANIZATIONS:
THOMAS, SPENCE
AND LIFE PHASES

Planning to write is not writing. Outlining…. researching…. talking to people about what you're doing, none of that is writing. Writing is writing.

E. L. Doctorow (1931 -)

There are other approaches then mine to memoir writing. My approach, as you now know, is to personalize your memoirs by identifying your own life stages.

Frank Thomas, my predecessor in teaching this course used what he called The Ladder of Life. Where I had seven stages Frank had ten steps to his ladder. Once you realize that Frank's first four steps equate to my first stage a striking similarity follows.

Frank promoted a memoir of ten chapters --- one for each step --- and asking students who wished to write a very detailed account of some episode to separate this story from the rest of the chapter and have it appear at the end of the chapter. Done in this manner the separated stories are called sidebars. If a reader was not interested in that amount of detail or that particular story it could be skipped without loss of continuity in the chapter. Thus a chapter was a survey for that period of your life.

Another memoir author by the name of Spence focused on major life changes to include nine of them.

STAGES FROM PUBLISHED BOOKS

		Number of Episodes
	HANSEN	
1	Birth Through High School (0-18)	22
2	College and Marriage Without Kids (18-22)	8
3	Starting a Family (22-27)	8
4	Early Family (27-39)	17
5	Middle Family (39-51)	14
6	Empty Nest and Grandchildren (51-57)	10
7	Retirement (58 and beyond)	<u>14</u>
		93
	THOMAS – The Ladder of Life	
1	Your Birth	
2	Your preschool childhood (0-5)	
3	Your elementary school years (5-13)	1
4	Your teen years (13-19)	
5	Your young adult years (19-25)	2
6	Your early marriage years (20-30)	3 & 4
7	Your early career years (20-35)	
8	Your middle years (35-55)	5
9	Your later years (55-65)	6
10	Your retirement years	7

How Hansen and Thomas Compare.

SPENCE *

1   Beginnings and Childhood

2   Adolescence

3   Early Adult Years

4   Marriage

5   Being a parent

6   Middle Adult Years

7   Being a Grandparent

8   Later Adult Years

9   Reflections

Legacy: A step-by-step guide to writing personal history
* by Linda Spence

Swallow Press
Ohio University Press
ISBN 0-8040-1002-1

Something helpful for regenerating details of your life is to identify your distinct life phases. Once done this aids in locating those one hundred short stories to be included in the memoir.

I have included my life phases as an example. Because of all my continual references to my wife and children I wish to take this time to apologize to those of you who never married and/or didn't have children. Please translate my comments as appropriate to best friend, partner, nieces, nephew, extended family, those legally adopted and those "adopted" by relationship.

Once I wrote out my life phases it was easy to identify stories for instance: for each child there is a birth story; graduation from high school story; marriage story and, perhaps, something unique like taking him to college or the bus terminal for military service.

Remember, everything I discuss is part of your buffet of ideas. If it is helpful and useful, great. Select what you want.

DISTINCT LIFE PHASES of Edmund Hansen

Ages

1-15	dependent on nuclear family
16-18	breaking away emotionally from nuclear family and confiding in friends instead
18-22	starting to live independent of nuclear family
16-30	dating, selecting a mate, higher education, military service, starting career and family
22-31	having children (first born to last born)
22-49	raising children (first born to last born out of high school)
41-49	launching children (high school graduation span)
46-51	marriages of children
51-57	empty nest while yet working
22-57	career
50-51 and 56-57	boomerang children
57- now	retirement: relocating to Florida, cruises, WI trips, Elderhosteling, writing, teaching memoirs
51-58	birth of grandchildren
59-	becoming the senior generation (both parents deceased)

Major Changes Affecting the Family

1963	Moving from Manitowoc to Oshkosh
1985	Finding out about Dean's homosexuality
1986	Leaving the family homestead
1992	Dean boomeranging back home with AIDS
1993	Dean's death and Lee's serious war injury
1994	Our move to Florida

ESSAY

Garrison Keillor

Clearing Up a Few Things

A family trip to a faraway place can help unlock the deepest of secrets

I HAVE BEEN RAMBLING AROUND BERLIN AND PARIS AND London with two brothers and a sister for two weeks, and it has actually been fun, for the simple reason that we had our fights long ago and don't need to have them again, and there was so much to talk about that we couldn't have with nonsiblings present, stuff from childhood when our hearts were open, and now we carry it everywhere we go. We were in London, having supper at the pub on the Thames where the gallows once stood where the highwayman Jack Sheppard swung back in the time of George I, and the river reminded us of the Mississippi, and pretty soon my brother was telling how he found a .32-cal. pistol in a cornfield behind the house when he was 15 and carried it around on his person for a few days because, he said, "I just liked the feel of it." He had no idea whether the gun was loaded or not.

I have known my brother for almost 60 years and he never told me this before. I guess the gallows was what reminded him of it. Now if our spouses or children had been there, they would have been bored silly long before the conversation got around to the pistol, and they'd have started talking about the reform of the House of Lords or something, but the truth is I am terribly interested in what happened in my childhood, there being fewer and fewer people left who remember it, and with siblings, your minds meld and you piece together the story of the big Keillor family meeting at our house in 1947—no need for footnotes or apology, you just sit down in Les Deux Magots café and hash it out, as French people of great elegance and purposefulness stride past, one of whom reminds you of your dad, a gray fedora on his head, smiling at the Revere movie camera as yellow streetcars rumble down Bloomington Avenue in 1953, and we children perk up and smile—someone off-camera has told us to smile, and like good children we do.

Or you walk up Unter den Linden to the Brandenburg Gate, and the great arch reminds you of Mother and Dad and how they eloped to Stillwater, Okla., and got married. (What year was that?) You walk into Parliament to meet your friend Matthew who grew up in a good leftist family and was made a peer by the Labour government, and you love to address him as Milord because it makes him wince, which reminds you of your history teacher Mr. Faust, and before long you are remembering Mr. Hochstetter and Miss Story and Miss Melby, who are clearer to you in London, being English teachers.

A person would like to get his life story together in coherent form, and life is not quite long enough to accomplish that, but a fact-finding trip with siblings is a big help. Those missing pieces in the puzzle that have been troubling you for years—Why did Dad carry a fire extinguisher when he went to the Boyds' to pick up Wanda for Sunday school? And your sister says, cool as can be, "Because Beryl Boyd was hopped up on vaporizers and liable to hallucinate and think that the house was burning down, and somehow a blast of liquid CO_2 seemed to calm her down." And there you have it. A little more of the story.

Over the years, my relatives have been cautious about sharing details of family history with me, knowing the business I'm in, knowing that writers are vacuum cleaners who suck up other people's lives and weave them into stories like a sparrow builds a nest from scraps. People meet writers and are bowled over when the writer is friendly to them and invites them to his house for a glass of wine or to shoot up heroin or whatever they do, and they talk their heads off, and a year later it comes out in a book, and there follow years of bitter and fruitless litigation, and that is why you should always keep a writer at arm's length. And that's all true.

But traveling to Europe relaxed my siblings, and they told me a lot of stuff I never knew before, and now I am pretty well set to talk about Lake Wobegon for at least two or three more years. And then I'll take them on a slow boat to China and find out more. What did my brother do with that .32-cal. pistol? What if it had been thrown into the cornfield by a heinous criminal? Or by Mr. Boyd, who had intended to blow Beryl's brains out and hid the weapon in the corn, and then went looking for it, and it wasn't there, and thus we were narrowly spared the tragedy? I would like to get this figured out. ■

TIME, APRIL 5, 2004

Some comments would be appropriate about sentence and paragraph length. When I wrote my first book my partner was a local reporter and the gal who did the editing was her editor. They quickly convinced me that shorter sentence length was preferred instead of numerous conjunctions or semi-colons.

They also stressed short paragraphs as opposed to the lengthier ones I was taught in school. Their reasoning wasn't contemporary writing style or anything similar. Instead they stressed the ease of reading. Shorter paragraphs give the reader more blank spaces on each page thus allowing them to complete a page sooner. Longer sentences and paragraphs tended to "bog" down and discourage the reader. I found myself adopting this style and I promote it to you.

To write long sentences requires a lot of talent to avoid the run-on sentence appearance. I provide one example of a 165 word sentence written by Garrison Keillor. But folks, this is difficult and I don't recommend his style.

May I add one more thought? Please, folks, keep it simple. Now I'll write more on this in the next chapter. All I want to say is --- don't try to impress the reader. Use, for memoir writing, the vocabulary used when speaking.

Now I don't claim to have the world's most extensive vocabulary. The following is the first paragraph of a book review, which appeared in The Tampa Tribune on Sunday, June 20, 2004.

'Jane Jacobs' 1961 classic, 'The Death and Life of Great American Cities', was a prescient and enormously influential jeremiad against the deadening fallout of modernist urban planning. But it was also an evocative ode to the messy cacophony of city life, a paean to the resilience and imagination of city dwellers.

Folks, this is where I stopped reading. It is pure crap. I don't read this sort of thing. She's only trying to impress and I'm not impressed. Don't do it.

CHAPTER TWELVE
MY PERSONAL GROWTH LEADING UP TO MY VIEWS ABOUT FOLK WRITING

Classic – a book people praise and don't read.

Mark Twain

When I was young I rebelled from parental dictates by not studying in school. I resented the continual comparison of me to my older brother who set the academic bar very high making it very difficult for me to compete.

As a senior in high school I began to realize I was hurting no one except myself and sensed the wisdom of my father who always said, "Get an education. Upwards mobility is dependent upon this principle. And it's important to rise above your roots." This sense of his wisdom represented growth for me and it was in time for me to salvage an education.

In college, as an undergraduate, I majored in both subjects in which I achieved success, those being Mathematics and Physics. I scorned English – especially literature – and the humanities, which seemed to have so much left to personal interpretation. Coming from a conservative family I grew up as a conservative young man and both science subjects represented stability, prestige or academic acceptance and a continuance of my conservative life. Finally I rejected Physics teaching because of the frustrating time spent in constant laboratory work with my inabilities in mechanical areas.

I did become a high school math teacher. This represented progress towards rising above my roots, accepting and living with my limitations and overcoming my youthful rebellion from parental comparison.

Eventually I realized – after becoming a university professor – that I didn't any longer need to pursue stability, prestige and continuance. I had them. In fact I became bored with mathematics and enjoyed the students more then the subject I was teaching. More personal growth.

Thinking another subject may reinvigorate my academic career I began studying accounting. Such terms as, "Generally accepted accounting principles" brought home to me how impure accounting was as an applied mathematics subject. Seeing applied math adapt to society instead of math explaining or interpreting the world around it was a growth reality check for me.

As a mathematician, your answers are either right or wrong. Right or wrong correlates to white or black in society. In mathematics your time is spent in the world of white while black represents a false try or start or incorrect answer.

The subject of accounting began to test my sense of right and wrong. Working as an accountant the areas of black and white are separated by a vast grey area where legal or illegal are yet to be defined by the courts.

While accounting professors are adamant about not functioning in the black they are equally adamant that you are not earning (or saving) your company all the money you could unless you are "pushing the envelope" and functioning in the grey area and as close to black as possible. Somehow this didn't mesh with my math training or my conservative upbringing.

My conservative family values are like those of the farmer cultivating his field, you stay between the lines. And if in doubt take the high road even if it means paying more taxes. That we don't need more people playing games to cheat the government. After all, the government works for us.

Thus accounting, as a profession, was not a match for me. I had learned more about me and my comfort zone for interacting with society.

With my health deteriorating I left mathematics teaching completely in 1986 and entered full time administration with the University's College of Business Administration. Suddenly I had to write letters, reports, etc., becoming what writers call a technocrat. How I wished to have studied my English back in college. Now I had to self-teach myself how to write. Ah yes, the folly of youth thinking they know how they will spend life. Does growth ever end?

Now I'm retired. So what do I do for my retirement? Play with my mathematics? Or Physics? I haven't looked at a physics book since 1958 and gave away every math book in 1986.

What I do is write. The very thing I hated most and tried to avoid while in college. This I say so that you realize that my comments about writing are my observations since my 1994 retirement. More growth.

I used to believe --- I'll swear I was taught this --- that sentences end with a period, exclamation mark or question mark. And this is the only time these three marks are used.

Then I read the sentence, "Are you going to the show?" said Mary. Oooops. Now I have a sentence with a question mark not at the end and a sentence within a sentence and thus is capitalized. More growth.

Shakespeare's writing and the story Bay-wolf (phonetic spelling) are earlier forms of the English language, which present – for me anyway – difficulty in understanding what is written. Then there are contemporary poems, which march to a different music. Does written English ever remain stable and constant? It is unlike mathematics. But I'm learning about how things evolve, about incorporating new words and changing the meaning of a word. More growth.

I'm at the point now where I tend to classify writing as classic, contemporary or Folk. Classic is the Shakespeare stuff which is still around after having passed the test of time – like good 'old' music; contemporary conforms to today's "generally accepted writing standards" – if you want a publisher to publish your work and have him pay for it this is what you use; and Folk.

Folk is the stuff we use in memoir writing because our primary concern is written story telling and the writing must pass the simple test of implanting your story from paper into the reader's mind. When it comes to grammar and spelling do not fret. It will be typed on a computer by you or someone else and much of this will be converted to contemporary writing. You may have to override the computer at times to maintain the flavor of the writing, especially if you want dialect.

The only law you have to follow is, as Dr. Phil says, "How's it working for you?" If you are getting the story into your reader's mind then, as a Folk writer, you are doing your job.

CHAPTER THIRTEEN
DISCUSS ADVERSITY

Nobody can write the life of a man, but those who have eat and drunk and lived in social intercourse with him.

Samuel Johnson

Some people want to write their memoirs on life's joys, fun, trips, good things that happened to them and end with aufweidersehn. Really now, is this life? No adversity? If you desire to leave a legacy of a life lived then how you dealt with life's adversities will communicate your true character.

I read once that: "Adversity merely presents the surface on which we render our soul's most exacting likeness. It is in the darkest skies that stars are best seen."

In the introduction to my memoirs will be found the following paragraph.

"Concerning the inevitable death of loved ones and other adversities, remember that the pleasures and successes of life are nice but character is hewn out of the adversities. It is not until I walked through the fires of life did I know what metal I was made of. Any memoir on only the 'good stuff' is simply self-promoting. It is necessary to disclose and discuss how I dealt with the 'hard stuff'; how I, with the support of others, picked myself up and moved on."

No one is immune from adversity. It's not if but when. The legendary Vince Lombardi said, "It's not whether you get knocked down; it's whether you get up."

In his book 'Losing Season' Pat Conroy writes: "There's no downside to winning", Conroy says. "Everyone loves it. You yell, spray champagne, guys get permission to hug. But losing is much more like life. Winning did nothing to help me when my mother died. Losing is preparation for the ups and downs of real life."

A memoir is incomplete without writing about your adversities. Examples of adversity include deaths of: grandparents, parents, siblings, spouse, and close friends. Others are loss of job, incapacitating illness, financial loss, fire, auto accident, etc. Most important is how the adversity impacted you and changed your life.

But does this mean writing about all the crap that happened to you or those around you? Or are you to be selective? Ah, read the next chapter.

CHAPTER FOURTEEN
NOT TELLING ALL

Writing books is the closest men come to childbearing.

Norman Mailer (1923 -)

When this course began I said I would tell what I did, why I did it and how I did it. So what is my experience writing sensitive things about family members? I'm glad you asked.

What Happened With My First Book

In my first book, 'A Father's Story', I discuss the polarization that occurred when we invited a non-celibate homosexual dying of AIDS to live his final days with us. This person was our son, Dean. Considering the polarizations I can identify three.

First our friends sorted themselves into two camps just like Moses dividing the Red Sea. There was no tweeners. Some, when they saw us coming, would do an about-face or cross to the other side of the street. The other group seemed to sense our despair and would come running with hugs and conversation.

Second was institutional distancing. Our church, when we were visiting Dean who was hospitalized in Phoenix, AZ and expected to die, prayed fervently for the three of us to have quality time and for the prolongation of life. But when their prayers were answered and we showed at our church with Dean we were quickly escorted to the door.

Thirdly was the fracturing of our family. The two sons living in Wisconsin – one in Oshkosh and the other fifty miles away in Green Bay – broke fellowship with Dean and as a result, with us. Only the son living 800 miles away in Virginia seemed to understand what was happening and flew back regularly on weekends to spend time with Dean.

Remember now that 'A Father's Story' was my method of grieving the death of a son. So did I write about the two sons who abandoned us when we brought Dean home? Certainly. After all they became part of the problem instead of part of our support system. If only they had cheered us on it would have been a tremendous help.

Did they like what I wrote about them? Absolutely not. But I needed to get EVERYTHING off my chest.

The story I wrote did everything possible to keep the door open for reconciliation. I used the metaphor of the prodigal son. The story of two sons and their father.

One son asked for his inheritance, left home and lived in the far country squandering his inheritance. Dean was this son. He was the brightest of the sons and this and his family values were the inheritance. He eventually lost everything.

The second son in the Biblical story was the stay-at-home son who worked along with his father.

When the prodigal son came home and the father welcomed him, the second son got his nose out-of-joint with his father's acceptance of him. Yes, this fits the two Wisconsin sons.

In the book, written in 1994 and published in 1996, I carefully wrote that while the problem occurred between the Wisconsin sons and me, the resolution would NOT be between them and me but them and their God. I hoped this would eliminate any need for contrition or eating of humble pie. Hopefully this would mean that we could go on with life. They could deal with the issue later and then not with me.

What have I learned? The lesson was learned only after I wrote a short story for Chicken Soup For The Writer's Soul in 1998. Here I also talked about the fracturing of the family. By the time the article was printed in the spring of 2000, we had repaired relations with one of the two sons. Yet in the article it sounded like this hadn't happened.

Writing about Dean is one thing – he is dead, his life's book is closed and not maturing or changing his views – but things written about living relatives is different. They represent moving targets. Their thinking will modify with time and positions once held likewise may change with the maturing process. Don't hinder this process by writing as final something which isn't.

My daughter-in-law chastised me for the Chicken Soup article because, by the time it was printed, it no longer reflected in 2000 what their situation was in 1993. It had changed and we were relating again. She was right. I was insensitive.

Things written are like inscriptions chiseled into granite. I would not change anything in A Father's Story because I had to grieve what happened but any further mention of the situation was very inconsiderate on my part and certainly not appropriate for a memoir. Anything written for memoirs should pass the test of not changing over time, not involve other people's personal business and be a legacy for further generations.

<u>Share At Your Comfort Level</u>

Remember, when reading my memoirs, that my wife and I underwent considerable counseling when we found out Dean had entered the homosexual lifestyle. In counseling it was stressed that openness is to health as secretiveness is to sickness. Thus my ability and willingness to share the intimacies of my life may not reflect what you wish or can share.

Find your own comfort level when writing your memoirs. You are doing this as a gift to your friends and relatives and should feel good about what is written. To feel compelled to include something you are uncomfortable with is not the way you want to go.

On the other hand, remember that most people seem hesitant to tell sensitive stories because they feel spotlighted and exposed. But humans are usually constrained by their own circumstances that when they read this about someone else they can relate to it and you have made a positive connection permitting them to be more honest with you.

What I Didn't Tell In My Memoirs

My wife has one brother. In high school he went to reform school; as a young adult he was in prison; as an older adult he had an addictive personality which contributed to: a sexual addiction, having multiple marriages, being an alcoholic and becoming a professional gambler which ruined him financially.

I have one brother who divorced his first wife and promptly remarried creating hard feelings within his own family and the extended family. The two children of the first marriage felt he abandoned them and their mother and to this day do not have a relationship they would otherwise have.

My mother-in-law was a controlling person, had low self-esteem, couldn't connect with people because she has no personality, had a dependent characteristic thus lived vicariously through others and was extremely self-centered all of which created a horrendously difficult life for my wife.

So what did I say about all this in my memories? Not one darn thing! I don't want other peoples lives messing up my memoirs. Remember, I lived a normal life in spite of these relatives. We did our best to not let their leaves blow in our yard. So why should I now?

My brother-in-law was very concerned that I was going to 'out' him since his daughter, grandkids and nieces and nephews would all receive copies of the book. Many of these people don't know his past.

The rule-of-thumb is to include your adversities – since this will communicate to the reader your true character – but you don't have to include all the baggage of those relatives who are mentioned in your memoirs. In fact, I would consider it inappropriate to include information on a personal level for any living relative.

Along this same vein don't lace your memoirs with bombs. If you are a homosexual don't 'out' yourself in your memoirs. Sexual indiscretions and other inappropriate behavior unknown to your relatives is best left that way.

If you are proud of earning your living as a strip dancer or being a Playboy model and this is common knowledge within the family, feel free to share this aspect of your life. I'm not trying to impose my morals on you. The bottom line is: Is it common knowledge already?

In my memoirs I wrote about the time I drank too many Hurricane Punch drinks while visiting the French Quarter in New Orleans. Soon I was on Bourbon Street directing traffic.

Is this something I'm proud of? Not particularly. But it was funny. Especially when two police officers decided I wasn't a public nuisance and just laughed as they walked by.

The common knowledge among my friends and relatives is that I love Martinis but I'm not a drunkard. What happened was not indicative of a more serious problem. I was trying to communicate that I'm a fun-loving person who, on this occasion, happened to drink too much. Knowing a slice-of-my-life is to know more of me. Some of the readers of my memoirs will only have my written word to know me by.

Bottom Line on Naming Names:
What Is Legally Libel or Defamation-of-Character?

By all means name those individuals who contributed to you becoming the person you are today. But be careful when you make disparaging comments.

Richard Burton's battle with booze was public knowledge, so wife Elizabeth Taylor could pen her struggles with Burton's demons with impunity. If your memoir reveals daddy dearest's secret sexual abuses, think twice before you publish them. Dishing dirt about private citizens can be cause for libel or defamation-of-character charges regardless of the truth. The libel test is, is it public knowledge and already published? Then it is in the public domain and you can write about it. Even if it is true but not public knowledge don't write about it without written permission.

Hiding a real person's identity behind a fictionalized name and description or using a real person's name to describe your childhood villain can get you into hot water, too. In the former case the issue is whether everyone knows the real name from the circumstances.

In my career memoirs some accused me of writing an expose! An expose is writing the truth others feel was best left unsaid. Nothing is illegal here, only the opinion of a few professors.

CHAPTER FIFTEEN
HOW TO ENGAGE THE READER: THE HOOK

Good writers are those who keep the language efficient.

Ezra Pound

How many times have you picked up a magazine, checked the contents page for an article that sounded interesting only to start reading and say, "This isn't interesting so let's see what other articles it has"? In short, the article didn't 'grab' you and you stopped reading after only reading a few paragraphs.

As you know by now my view of memoirs is that it is a collection of short stories the composite of which is your life story. Each episode is a short story publishable in its own right and thus the rules of engagement for short story writing apply. What I'm saying is each episode must 'grab' the reader by the end of the first two or three paragraphs. So how do you do this?

Allow me to provide ten examples to illustrate how to 'grab' the reader. Professionally, this is called the 'hook'.

First example:

Turn to page 298 of my memoirs. The episode starts after WE REMEMBER CHRISTMAS 1992 WELL.

Notice that the first paragraph places you the reader into the story. Its like I'm across the table telling the story.

The second paragraph should begin to arouse your interest. Why is my wife pouring out her soul – and to a support group at that? It also hints at a man whom you suspect will play a part in the story or he wouldn't be mentioned.

The third paragraph should leave you thinking, "What so moved this stranger to donate $2000?"

The fourth paragraph indicates that someone will die.

Starting with the fifth paragraph the writing is narrative to tell the story chronologically starting a year earlier.

Alright. Are you hooked into reading the rest of the story?

Second example:

Turn to page 22 and start with the last paragraph on this page.

The first paragraph of the story is designed to place you in a darkened living room looking out the window for air raid wardens. This should create suspense where, when and how eminent is the danger?

Third example:

Turn to page 34 and the first paragraph following the comment about the article being published December 1, 1998.

The first thirteen paragraphs were designed to have you walk along with me delivering papers on a cold winter evening. Many men of my generation delivered papers after school and thus would be experiencing 'memory sparklers' upon reading this. The women of my generation will have memories of brothers and sons involved with similar experiences.

It's not until the fourteenth paragraph, the one starting 'My father was one of eleven…' that background is provided. As Paul Harvey would say, "Now for the rest of the story".

Notice that the first example involving Christmas 1992 raised questions in your mind. The second example, the WWII story involved suspense while the third example is 'Walk awhile with me'. But all three are written so as to engage the reader.

Fourth example:

Turn to page 167 and start at the top of the page.

The first fifteen paragraphs involve story telling. This is what I actually did one January. I think everyone enjoys a good story if well told or written.

Certainly I wanted more about my Cub experience then just a story. The fifteenth paragraph ends – "Boy is it smoky in here and does it ever stink". This is where the scope of the story is broadening out.

The engagement of the reader – a good story.

Fifth example:

Go to page 164 and start at the top of the page.

The first eight paragraphs are all dialogue. You become a listener to a conversation between my wife and her doctor right after giving birth to our fourth son.

After eight paragraphs the 'rest of the story' is told. Hopefully by then you are also saying, "What? A baby holding a birth control pill!"

The engagement of the reader – eaves-dropping on a private conversation.

Sixth example:

Is on page 383 starting with 'Exotic Cruises—'

The first two paragraphs are simply far out humor. If you know me you realize this is characteristic Edmund Hansen. And your writing should reflect your personality.

After the first two paragraphs I get more serious and discuss my retirement activities.

The engagement of the reader – dialogue and a fictional tail.

Remember that just because you use quotation marks indicating dialogue – something said by someone – great latitude is accepted as part of dramatic license. The essence of the story is correct. People were questioning me on why I wanted to travel to the Baltic Sea instead of, say, the Mediterranean Sea, which contained countries that are the origin of western civilization; or the Holy Land. These people didn't know how much my uncles and aunts talked about Denmark and a few having made a pilgrimage back to Kollenberg, Denmark to see the church where Grandpa and Grandma were married.

Seventh Example:

Is on page 15, starting at the top.

The first two paragraphs is dialogue between my mother and Doctor Swanton. Is this what was actually said? I certainly was present that day but hadn't yet learned English. But my parents told me the story dozens of times that I was supposed to be a girl. The dialogue, I'm sure, is close to what was said; close enough to be the essence of the conversation.

The engagement of the reader – dialogue designed to make the reader part of the unfolding drama.

Eighth example:

Is the article written by Harold Allison of Sun City Center, which appeared November 11, 2003 in The Tampa Tribune. It was part of a series honoring WWII memories.

"I was hustled out of the barracks and into the snow with the rest of the American POWs of Stalag 3A. I was a lot shorter than most of the men, and from my place in the rear, I could not see or hear what was going on up front, nor could I be seen. Some bales of hay were stacked nearby, so I climbed on top of them for a better view. When I got it, I breathed a heartfelt prayer: "Thank God I'm short!"

"Drafted 60 years ago, when I turned 18 in ---"

This is enough to make my point. No man wants to be short so something traumatic is about to happen. The hook is suspense – you want to know what happened.

Ninth example:

Is the article written by Don Looper of Sun City Center and teacher in our Community College. It appeared in The Tampa Tribune January 6, 2004 as part of the I Remember It Well series.

"There she sits, graceful as ever, pushing 80 but still able to command $10,000 for a night's work. She hasn't lost her good looks or her appeal to history lovers. Still, a lady of her vintage cannot forever deny her years, and the Sequoia yearns for a new home, where she can retire with the respect she deserves as a National Historic Landmark"

I'm sure you agree: WOW, WHAT A WOMAN. Of course a picture of a ship accompanied the article and all seamen realize that ships are referred to in the feminine.

The next paragraph starts:

"The Sequoia had her ups and downs after Jimmie Carter banished her in 1977..."

Don's elegant writing – his wordmanship – alone is sufficient to cause you to want to continue. His affectionate 'her', 'pushing 80', 'night's work', 'good looks', 'lady of her vintage', 'respect she deserves' are very descriptive. Reading the writings of a polished writer is always a pleasure.

Tenth example:

Is my 2004 Christmas paradigm of the famous 'Tis The Night Before Christmas'.

In a paradigm a separate hook is not necessary. But the story of which your article is a paradigm must be a universally recognized story. Certainly this very famous story fits these criteria.

As the reader proceeds he should be looking for how verses are treated in the contemporary drama.

A Christmas Gift Of Love Drives A Need For Speed

By EDMUND HANSEN
Special to the Tribune

SUN CITY CENTER — 'Twas the night before Christmas, and nothing was stirring because my wife and I were attending a special midnight Christmas Eve church service.

We were entranced by the drama unfolding, yet tired, ready to entertain those sugarplum dreams. But suddenly, within my wife's belly, there arose such activity that she knew in an instant her time had just come.

Silently, she wrote: "We must leave NOW!"

With all eyes upon us, I helped my pregnant wife waddle up the aisle and placed her on a bench by the outer front door. I then ran for our car.

Soon she was seated next to me, and we drove to our house to retrieve her packed suitcase. As we walked back to the car, my wife exclaimed, "Oh no! My water just broke!"

This was not our first child, so we knew what this meant. Urgency was now the essence of all our activity as our child served notice of starting his descent.

Few cars were on the road, permitting me to speed like the down of a thistle. Stopping neither for stop signs nor red lights, I couldn't

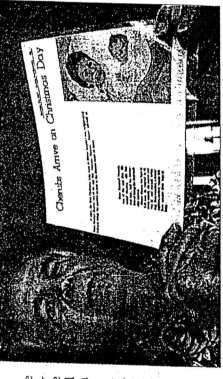

Tribune photo by ROBERT BURKE

Potholes, red lights and freight trains couldn't stop Edmund Hansen from getting his wife to the hospital on Christmas Eve in 1963, just in time for the birth of their son Dean. It was a very special Christmas present, and one never forgotten, the proud father says.

help thinking how helpful Rudolph would have been.

Speeding did produce one complication. I either soundly hit potholes or swerved to miss them, rocking the car. Either activity resulted in my wife muttering unpleasant sounds. How we could have used Santa's cloud-cushioned sleigh!

Approaching the only railroad tracks in town, I suddenly saw the red warning lights start blinking and the crossing guards lowering.

And would you believe it was a long, slow-moving freight train? What to do?

I turned to my wife and said, "Can you wait?" Her response reverberated off the roof of the car: "Yeeeee-owie-eesss."

I didn't like that answer and resorted to action, realizing that any action would give the impression of progress in the making.

I sped down the street both parallel and opposite to the direction the train was heading, then zoomed across the tracks at the first intersection after the caboose passed. While this added slightly to the distance, I do believe we saved precious seconds, and the action engaged my wife. It also made me feel like I was doing something.

Pulling up to the emergency entrance, we were welcomed by many helping "elves." As a nurse was wheeling Ginny to the delivery room, the nurse said, "Here comes our first Christmas baby!" And our third son, Dean, was just that. It was a very special Christmas present and one never forgotten.

The next morning, I looked skyward, half expecting to see Santa in his sleigh pulled by eight miniature reindeer saying, "Merry Christmas to all, and to all, a good night."

Edmund Hansen's son, Dean, born on Christmas Day in 1963, died in 1993 of AIDS. Hansen and his wife retired six months later to Sun City Center, where Hansen says he followed his son's lead and took up writing. A former university math professor, he has since written a book about his son's illness, a short story for "Chicken Soup for the Writer's Soul" and other stories.

CHAPTER SIXTEEN
THE WORLD AROUND US: CIVIL RIGHTS

The pen is the tongue of the mind.

Miguel DeCervantes (1547-1616)

On pages 140 and 141 of my memoirs I discuss the broad picture of the civil rights issue and how it degenerated into thousands of riots. How in the 1960's and early 1970's this issue engulfed the nation. It was impossible for anyone living in this country at that time to not be affected. The issue really struck home with me when the University of Wisconsin-Oshkosh, the college I attended and later taught for 31 years, erupted November 21, 1968 into a full blown race riot which closed down the campus.

This is one of those things not to be ignored in memoirs. I grew up in a family that was very prejudicial against Black people even though none lived in Appleton, Wisconsin. Contemplating this in adulthood I believe I have the answer; ask me if you're curious.

I chose not to treat this as an episode since it permeated my entire life. This is one of those principles given to me as a starting point by my family of origin which required updating and growth on my part throughout my lifetime. At some point I had to say, "And what do I believe". It was necessary for me to move away from my parent's belief and be accountable as a human being.

My approach in writing about this was to start with my parents admonition about Black people and carry this to the point where in my final job at the university, one of my best buddies – a most loyal assistant – was a Black man.

Turn to page 53 and 54.

Under Father's Philosophy the second paragraph reads: "After all, I could have been born in a country that wouldn't allow class mobility, or born to a family with no ambition, or born Black or Native American. Please, this is not a racial statement but a realization that Whites in the U.S. have had advantages not available to Blacks or to Native Americans, or those born in poverty regardless of race."

The tenth point reads:

"Birds of the same feather flock together. You don't see a robin mating with a bluebird to you? God never meant for Black people and White people to marry -----."

There are times when I say, "Ed, don't be too critical of your father. After all he was only reflecting contemporary thought. It wasn't until 1967 – thirteen years after you graduated from high school – that the Supreme Court ruled the state laws banning marriages between individuals of different races were unconstitutional." Then my self-talk says, "If Adam and Eve are the world's first couple and the human race descended from them then where does he think Black people came from?"

I do love my father and am very thankful that he gave me a set of principles to start life with. As I said before, at some point we are responsible for our own life principles and give credit where credit is due with forgiveness for the rest. At some point we make up for our own deficiencies to sail our ship.

Turn to page 71 – the fifth paragraph down reads:

"When stationed at Norfolk Naval Yard a few of us visited Jamestown and Colonial Williamsburg. We were impressed by all that we saw but the one thing that shocked me was seeing 'White Only' and 'Colored Only' signs outside restrooms. I had read about this but seeing is believing."

Turn to page 86 – the last paragraph. Please start reading and continue through the first five paragraphs on page 88.

This was the first time I had intimate contact with a Black man.

Turn to page 99. Read that page and the first three paragraphs on page 100. We were shocked to find discrimination even in language. Turn to page 140 and read chapter 8C (pages 140-152). This covers the race riot at the University of Wisconsin-Oshkosh.

Turn to page 328 and read the episode entitled: Morris Hampton. His picture will be found on page 321.

Civil Rights is the only issue integrated into episodes and not a stand-alone episode.

CHAPTER SEVENTEEN
CREATIVITY IN MEMOIR WRITING: WHAT OTHERS DID

The man who does not read good books has no advantage over the man who can't read them.

Mark Twain (1835 – 1910)

From Grandson to Grandfather by Edmund Hansen

I want to stress that my memoir is a dual memoir. In my introduction I write:

"Men of my generation lived two lives: the family man and the career or working man. Any memoir of me would be incomplete if my career and its' achievements plus trials and tribulations were not included. This was a large part of my life and to know me, in addition to knowing the family man, is to understand my relationship to work. Work was how I contributed to society and how I earned the money to feed my family."

I go on to say that the text is written with separate chapters for the career man. These have a 'C' after the chapter number. For those who want just the family man, the 'C' chapters could be skipped without losing continuity of the family man.

From The Ends Of The Earth by A.H. Felman

Dr. Felman is a retired pediatrician living in Brandon.

In the course of living a life to old age we all can reflect back and see 'turning points' and 'forks in the road'. Once a direction or path is chosen usually there is no turning back to restart life by taking the other choice. Major life decisions are not reversible.

I'm sure everyone, upon reflection, says: "what if I had taken the other path?" We'll never know but Dr. Felman did speculate about a decision point in his life.

Dr. Felman was a man living on the East Coast who was programmed by his parents to be a medical doctor. At age 18 he hitchhiked to California for a vacation; this being the summer after high school just before attending his freshman year of college.

Having insufficient time to hitchhike back he took a bus for the return trip. In Tulsa, Oklahoma he had a layover. This is when he reflected on whether or not to return home and study medicine. Remember that this memoir was written after Dr. Felman retired when people are inclined to ask, "What if I ---".

In writing his memoirs he creates a fictional self who takes the other path – dude ranching.

Dr. Felman does return to his home and the life for which he was programmed.

Now, in the book he develops a dual path; his real memoirs and the fictional person who will live out the other life. He carries this out to the end of the book when he, Dr. Felman, meets his fictional self while vacationing with his wife at the dude ranch owned by his fictional self.

Very unique and very creative.

The Medic and The Mama-san by Michael Hall

I met Mike in February of 1996 at the St. Petersburg International Folk Fest. As a sponsor of refugees from Southeast Asia I instinctively headed for the Vietnamese area. As I picked up a book from a pile the attendant said, "If you want to talk to the author he's over there," pointing to a Caucasian dressed in traditional Vietnamese clothing.

We conversed at length discussing our shared interest in writing. My book, A Father's Story was scheduled for an April release and he asked that I send him the first copy – which I did; also enclosing a note saying "Let's get together again." He responded by phone and he and wife, Minh, showed up a few days later carrying a bottle of Sangria wine.

Mike wasn't retired yet and they were expecting Minh's family from Vietnam any day. We decided not to pursue a friendship until after Minh's family was settled. When I attempted to re-establish contact three years later he was in the final stage of colon cancer.

So what makes Mike's book unique? It's a dual memoir of Mike and Minh until they met in Vietnam. By dual I mean Mike alternated chapters writing a few years of his life followed by Minh's for the same period. Minh was not literate even in her own language so everything was written by Mike, who was an excellent writer.

Mike was a medic in Vietnam and Minh a domestic worker in hootch number 11. Mike lived in hootch number 9. The book covers their upbringing, courtship, marriage and the trials and tribulations getting Minh to this country. It was Minh who said to Mike, "You must preserve our story for our children".

Mike and Minh have given numerous talks to Vietnam groups, VFW's, schools and community groups for awareness and to help mending grieving souls. He has had at least two printings and, like me, has his own publishing operation called Hawkeye Publishing, named after the TV program MASH.

Edmund Hansen

"Root – Hog or Die" by James H. Oettel

What motivates a man to complete his memoirs? Is it education? Unique experiences such as travel, military or a special job? Or great facility in writing?

The answer is none of the above. Certainly having them is nice and helpful but not necessary.

James Oettel enrolled in my memoirs class in the fall of 2003. He was already well along writing his memoirs.

Born in 1929 to poor parents at the start of the depression things went from bad to desperate. He lived under bridges, in the open on the ground and at age four in a cave for 18 months. The family frequented soup lines, begged and went without for food. They walked from state to state looking for work living in Pennsylvania, Washington D.C., Louisiana, Florida, Texas, Missouri and all points between. Occasionally they were able to collect enough money to ride a bus or train.

At the age of 12 both Jim's parents died within two weeks of each other and still Jim survived to write about it. Almost blind from malnutrition he still served in the Army Air Force and obtained other jobs by paying another to take the physical for him.

Jim has an intestinal fortitude unlike any other I've seen. This drive to stay alive, root-hog or die, is what provided the strength to complete his memoirs while others with many advantages are still working.

Jim self-published his memoirs through a Publish-On-Demand publisher by the name of AuthorHouse. A flat fee is paid by the author to load his materials into the computer, for formatting, the I.S.B.N. number and for handling distribution. His book may be obtained from: Amazon.com, Barnes and Noble.com and AuthorHouse.com.

I include his book in this manual because despite not even a high school education he DID IT!

He is the quintessential memoirist utilizing folk art writing.

Achieving variety can also be done by including the following:

1. Poetry

2. Family sayings

3. Quoting from family letters

4. Recipes

5. A family tree

6. Humor

7. Photos

8. Dialogue

9. Clippings

10. Quotes from a diary

11. Statistics: price of car, home; population

12. Maps

13. Calligraphy

14. Vital documents: birth certificates, immigration papers

15. Famous proverbs, Bartlett's quotations

16. Drawings

17. Family anecdotes

18. Dialect

19. A chronology – your life in brief (beginning)

20. Lyrics of a song

21. Names of people

22. Special awards

23. Titles

24. See from Grandson to Grandfather on the following pages 116-117, 148, 323, 329, 338-341

CHAPTER EIGHTEEN
WRITING TOOLS

The greatest thing in style is to have a command of metaphor.

Aristotle (384 – 322 B.C.)

As a craftsman you need tools. Likewise as a storyteller you need to hone your writing skills utilizing the tools of the storyteller trade.

<u>Metaphor</u>

We all tend to use analogies in our conversation to draw a comparison between two similar or dissimilar things. An example would be to draw a comparison between self-confidence and speaking ability.

A metaphor is a figure of speech comprised of a word or phrase that transfers its meaning to another use such as: we are 'drowning in paperwork' is a metaphor and not meant to be taken literally.

Webster's Dictionary says: A figure of speech in which a term is transferred from the object it ordinarily designates to an object it may designate only by implicit comparison or analogy, as in the phrase 'evening of life'.

In the metaphor 'to throw me to the wolves' clearly doesn't literally mean what it says but someone or something is just as ravenous and destructive as wolves. Likewise, 'the ping-pong table was the one field on which the civil war raged openly' means that the struggle between the players was as hostile and as deadly serious, at least to the players.

There are a few do's and don'ts with metaphors. First of all avoid heavily used metaphors like: "avoid like the plague", "pretty as a picture", "quiet as a mouse", "hungry as a bear". Effective figurative language constantly seeks new comparisons instead of recycling old ones. "Avoid like a tax audit" is much better than "avoid like the plague".

Secondly don't be too original. If carried too far, the original becomes the bizarre. Unless you're writing comedy, "Mary's heart melted like a glacier under accelerated global warming" is a stretch.

Don't mix metaphors as in, "Sam tried hard at the debate club, but the thrusts of his argument were usually fruitless". Thrusts and fruitless are confusing to the reader. The following, "Sam tried hard at the debate club, but the point of his argument usually ended up blunted". 'Point' and 'blunted' work well together.

And finally make sure your metaphor agrees with your story. If you are writing about cavemen days and then write, "Suddenly the girl's thoughts derailed like a freight train hitting a sharp bend" you don't have congruency between 'cavemen' and 'freight trains'.

Some metaphors are regional. My wife traveled to Sydney, Australia and was shown a bridge connecting the sides of the bay. A crew of workers has a permanent full time job painting the bridge starting on one side of the bay, ending on the other side and then repeating the process. In Sydney a metaphor for an endless task is to say, "It's like painting the bridge".

I enjoy looking for metaphors. One day I heard TV commentators discussing the 9-11 commission hearings. The following were metaphors used to stress that President Bush needed to obtain more information: "pulse the agencies", "butt heads", "connect the dots" and "shake the trees".

Listening to Good Morning America (ABC 7-9 A.M. daily) I heard a conversation about why the Democrats were bringing up President Bush's National Guard duty during the Vietnam War. One said they are, "Letting the President know they intend to play hard ball". Another said they are, "Testing the market". Then George Stephanopoulos said it was, "A brush back pitch".

Metaphors found in my memoirs include:
rose colored glasses
the kaleidoscope of my life
the salt-and-pepper of the earth
buffet of courses

Life is like a hand in a card game. You have no choice in what cards are dealt. But I have a hell-of-a lot to say about how I will play those cards.

Birth of children is like a potluck meal. You take whatever is given to you.

Edmund Hansen

__Simile__

Similes and metaphors are word constructions in which one thing is presented as being like another thing. Similes use "like" or "as" to make this point. Examples would include "Fay was in her fifties, short, stocky and as muscular as a longshoreman" and "The water was coated with the bilge oil of numerous ships, filth that would not evaporate in the low temperature and left a black ring on the rocky walls of the fjord as though from the bath of a slovenly giant".

The main advantage of this type of writing is the creation of a striking visual impression on the reader. "Fay was in her fifties, short and stocky" is an adequate description, but not nearly as memorable. Try going through each sentence above removing the figurative language. I'm sure you will agree that the result is less vivid.

Similes and metaphors appeal to people who like to play with language for its own sake. But are they really different? I'm sure a purest would say yes; that they are both sub-categories of analogies in general and separate from each other in particular.

Personally I view similes as a sub category of metaphors; that is, a special kind of metaphor. As such you will seldom hear me say 'simile' but refer to everything of this type as a 'metaphor'.

Clichés and Proverbs

Many memoir teachers feel strongly about limiting the use of clichés. That phrases like: "cool as a cucumber", "light as a feather" or "like two peas in a pod" have become stale phrases. In fact many consider clichés as worn out metaphors. Well, that may be true if these phrases are over used but as memoirists it is important to use the language of the period you are writing about so: do it. It may be worn out in today's vernacular but weren't in the period you're writing about.

Clichés are a fact of life. They become imprinted in the recesses of your mind. My mother was diagnosed with Alzheimer's disease and confined to a nursing home for her last seventeen years. Early on in her disease, while she could still talk, her language began to digress into nothing but clichés --- dated clichés from her early adult years and finally into early youth. I could actually see her language backing up decade by decade. Friends have told me of similar experiences. Perhaps clichés have picked up a 'bad rap' from people experiencing as I the ravages of this deadly disease.

In the book The Dictionary of Clichés by James Rogers, the author says: "The cliché has a bad name as an overworked and therefore banal expression. Spoken or written by someone who is not thinking much about what he is saying or writing, it usually upholds that reputation. Among people who do pay attention to their phrasing, however, clichés can serve as the lubricant of language: summing up a point or a situation, easing a transition in thought, adding a seasoning of humor to a discourse----

"Doubtless as you look through this book you find sayings that strike you as proverbs. Many of them are. Since proverbs represent the distilled wisdom from decades or centuries of human experience, it is small wonder that many of them become fixtures of the language. If you were to leaf through The Oxford Dictionary of English Proverbs, however, you would find more unfamiliar than familiar entries, since as time passes many proverbs by overwork caused them to lose favor. The distinction I have made between proverb and cliché is current use: if a proverb still gets heavy duty in the language, it ranks as a cliché".

Clichés found in my memoirs include:

page 266	"…one brick short of a load"
page 266	"He was not playing with a full deck."
page 267	"…his dipstick didn't touch the oil"
page 267	"…screw loose"
page 271	"His lights are on but nobody is home."
page 276	"…one can short of a six-pack"
page 270	"…our leaves blow in your yard"

This extensive use of clichés in Chapter 16 was for affect. It was the language used in the mid 80's.

Parable

This is a story that illustrates a moral lesson. It really is a stand-alone metaphor. By stand-alone I mean a story in its own right.

The parables we are most familiar with are those told by Jesus and written in the Bible. In some cases the moral is couched in a story simply to avoid the wrath of the Roman government. On other occasions they were actual stories with a setting in time, place and culture. An understanding of this setting is necessary to obtain meaning from its analogy to our twenty-first century situation.

Slang

This is something we all know; yet it is very hard to define. Some definitions range from: illegitimate colloquial speech; the language of low, illiterate or disreputable persons; to plain man's poetry. The American poet Carl Sandburg defined it, "_ _ _ language that rolls up its sleeves, spits on its hands and goes to work_ _ _". Henry Buckle called it language serving its apprenticeship.

Slang is not in fact jargon, a secret code, unacceptable usage or the idiom of everyday speech, catchphrases, journalese, buzzwords, or idiolect (the private language of an individual).

From a linguist's point of view, slang is a style category within the language, which occupies an extreme position on the spectrum of formality. Slang is at the end of the line where language is considered too racy, raffish, novel or unsavory for use in conversation with strangers.

Slang also functions within social sub-groups, ranging from surfers, school children and yuppies, to criminals, drinkers and fornicators.

Should you use slang in memoir writing? Yes but limit the use. Some slang will date your writing. Thus the use of slang may be for that purpose alone. I call it vintage writing.

My Uncle Carl always used the slang word 'doozy' which is also spelled 'dooze'. He said in Chapter 1 of his memoirs "_ _ _ that the exploding firecrackers scared the milkman's horse _ _ _ was a doozy of a firecracker". I always knew what he meant but it wasn't a word in my vocabulary with my circle of friends.

Later in life I learned that the origin of the word was the pre-World War II car called the Duesenburg a very expensive car – the best of everything. My friends and me would have said it was the 'cadillac' of firecrackers. The Cadillac was the best and most expensive car of my growing up days.

While doozy will date your writing it is a word still seen today and is defined in Webster's Dictionary as slang meaning something extraordinary.

Slang which appears in my memoirs include: bamboozle; pipe dreaming; all schnorkered up; hogwash; dumbfounded; Yea, sure, you betcha; flabbergasted; computereze; whatchamacallit; Yadda, yadda; thingamajig; doohickey; bimbo. These were the words of my vocabulary and are authentic Edmund Hansen. Certainly some of it dates me, like pipe dreaming – meaning smoking marijuana. This is a '60s expression while 'smoking a turkey' was used in the '80s.

Should you be of the opinion that current press is above slang allow me to list a few which appeared either in The Tampa Tribune or Time magazine during this past year.

harangued	whatsisname	gallivanting
riffraff	whosits	numskull
overous	whatchacallem	pet peeve
lackadaisical	mealy mouth	batty
whatyoucallit	putrid	loose cannon
whatcha	kaput	rocket scientist
goddammit	skullduggery	dagnabit
whining	snafu	tarnation
blaguarding	fuhgetaboutit	doink doink
jumping jchosesphats		persnickety
bada bing	one-trick-pony	lotta
schmoozer	kerplunk	didya
swaggered	guffaws	stoopid
baksheesh (a gratuity)		ding-a-ling
outa	brouhaha	pooh-poohed
hodgepodge	head honcho	snazzy

Euphemism

This is a mild or vague or periphrastic (pronounced per-e-fras-tik meaning the use of a longer phrasing in place of a possible shorter form) expression as a substitute for blunt precision or disagreeable truth. Examples include:

heck instead of hell
flip your lid instead of go mad
fly a kite instead of get lost
bologna instead of bull shit (and I don't mean cow dung but liar)

One of our sons would say "student discount plan" when not leaving a sufficient tip in a restaurant. To use a metaphor, a rose by any other name smells the same. In other words, he was stealing from the waitress. If you can't afford the tip don't eat in the restaurant.

Other commonly used euphemisms are: Five finger discount for shop lifting and light fingered for a pick-pocket (someone who steals a wallet).

<u>Hyperbole</u>

Be sure to distinguish this word from hyperbola which in mathematics is a plane curve with well-defined properties.

By this point in the course you have heard me say that if you tell a lie large enough that nobody believes you then you haven't lied, just told a 'whale' of a story. Lying is the intentional spoken falsehood with the purpose of deceiving the recipient. And if the recipient is deceived then, and only then, is a lie spoken. If no one is deceived only a 'tall' tail was spoken.

The hyperbole is a spoken exaggeration used for effect to dramatize the point – never believed in its own right.

Examples include:
I'm so hungry I could eat an elephant.
She's as big as a whale.
She's as big as a house.
Chocolate is to die for.
Crawling in bed with the enemy.
Knock his socks off.
Let the fox in the hen house.

Idiom

This is the assigning of a new meaning to a group of words which already have their own meaning in conversational American English. Examples include:

cool cat
fly off the handle
to get away with something
to take it easy   relax

rest

not to worry

pepper and salt   streaks of gray hair

mixed marriage

time off
kick the bucket
don't count your chickens before they're hatched
caught between the devil and the deep blue sea
seize the bull by the horns
to be up the creek
tut-tut
put the candy back

<u>Oxymoron</u>

This is a pair of words which are inherently contradictory. Like saying: 'honest politician' or 'honest used car salesmen'. Talking about athletes from, say, Florida State where their graduation rate is 20% the term 'intelligent athlete' is an oxymoron. (I hope you don't mind my humor.)

Last March 20, 2004 I was stopped dead in my tracks by a headline in The Tampa Tribune. It said "Meat-eating Vegetarians—".

Once I read the article I realized the writer used an oxymoron to grab your attention because your immediate thought is, a meat-eater is not a vegetarian. The article was about vegetarians who are not 100 percent committed. They are part-time vegetarians. People who have greatly reduced their meat eating.

Historic Expressions which have taken on a **contemporary** **meaning** where the original meaning is lost.

This is similar to idiom except few people remember the historic meaning. Examples include:

        sleep tight and don't let the bed bugs bite

        raining cats and dogs

*   pulling your leg

        big wig

        undertaker

        left holding the bag

        to rake over the coals

*   big shot

        don't have an inkling

        to turn the tables

        chairman

*   mind your P's and Q's

        from soup to nuts

        puttin' on the dog

        half-cocked

        lock, stock and barrel

        cold shoulder

caught with hand in the till

* black-balled

upper crust

flip your wig

to go whole hog

to go the whole nine yards

* rule of thumb

face the music

blue moon

flash-in-the-pan

square meal

son-of-a-gun

cut the red tape

* cold enough to freeze the balls off a brass monkey

* explanation provided

To write out the original meaning of these examples – and this is not a complete list – is more than you want to read. But allow me to provide six examples so you get the flavor of what I'm saying.

black balled

In many elections, voters used black and white balls placed in a wooden chest to cast their vote for someone. Receiving all black balls meant failure due to "black balling". Such a system was used by George Washington and other Patriots at the Rising Sun Tavern in Fredericksburg, Virginia at lodge meetings.

a big shot

This phrase comes from the English proclivity to shoot off the big guns or cannons and illuminate the town with candlelight in every window whenever a VIP arrived in town.

mind your P's and Q's

Tavern keepers and tavern wenches (female servants) reminded colonials to watch their pints and quarts of ale when they judged that they might have had too much to drink.

Another explanation I heard was from the printing business. Before printing the type had to be set by hand. These being long rectangular pieces of lead with the letter on the end. The P's and Q's were side-by-side and looked much the same. Thus printers had to watch their P's and Q's.

rule of thumb

In colonial times women were considered the actual property of their husbands upon marriage. By law, the husband was allowed to beat his wife with anything in diameter smaller than his thumb. If she could prove that she was beaten with something larger than his thumb, she could haul him into court and press charges. If convicted, the sentence would likely be a stint in the stocks or pillory or possibly to have his ears nailed to the pillory post from sun up to sundown.

son-of-a-gun

Sailors on British 17th century ships-of-the-line allowed wives on board when in port. When giving birth (sailors lived around their cannons) sometimes the gun was fired to help the women push harder. These children were called son-of-a-gun.

cold enough to freeze the balls off a brass monkey

In the heyday of sailing ships, all war ships and many freighters carried iron cannons. Those cannons fired round iron cannon balls. It was necessary to keep a good supply near the cannon, but prevent them from rolling about the deck. The best storage method designed was a square based pyramid with one ball on top, resting on four resting on nine, which rested on sixteen. Thus, a supply of thirty cannon balls could be stacked in a small area right next to the cannon.

There was a problem – how to prevent the bottom layer from sliding and rolling from under the others. The solution was a metal plate called a 'monkey', with sixteen round indentations. If this plate was made of iron, the iron balls would quickly rust to it. The solution to the rust problem was to make "Brass Monkeys".

Few landlubbers realize that brass contracts much more and much faster than iron when chilled. Consequently, when the temperature dropped too far, the brass indentations would shrink so much that the cannon balls would come right off the monkey. Thus, it was quite literally "cold enough to freeze the balls off a brass monkey!" This is very different then contemporary usage.

pulling your leg

One popular meaning originated during a public hanging when the condemned person was still somehow alive after props had been knocked out from underneath. It was then that the jailor reached up and pulled the prisoner's leg hard enough to break the leg, thus preventing the prisoner from pushing up for air, resulting in suffocation.

Dialogue

If we meet in the mall unexpectedly, our conversation will start like:

"Hi"

"Well hello. How are you?"

"Oh I'm okay. What have you been doing lately?"

Notice how we ping-pong back and forth sharing the conversation. I often call this 'love making'. We all do it. This is how we typically get the conversation underway. But it's not until "_ _ _ been doing lately" is there any substance.

Don't include this type of conversation in memoir writing. It's too boring. Get beyond it by saying something like, 'After exchanging pleasantries, Mary said _ _ _'

Dialogue is to be an integral part of the story and not to 'mark time'. It is extremely useful in starting a story for engaging the reader immediately with the ongoing drama. But remember, dialogue slows the story to the same pace as though two people were actually conversing. Whereas narrative can move the story along for one thousand years in a single sentence.

Capturing humor is also one of the capabilities of dialogue.

Is dialogue fact or truth?

Jan Muna writes in Memoir Writing:

"If your memoir is being written for publication, you don't want it to be full of rambling reminiscences. You want episodes, scenes brought to life with vivid details of the place, the time, the people present. You want to include dialogue. And, of course, it must be true. And that becomes difficult. What is truth? Have you ever discussed an event with a family member or an old friend and discovered that each of you remembered it somewhat differently? Each person sees it through different eyes, bringing a different set of values or feelings to it. Therefore, the truth that you are writing is your truth. What you saw, what you heard, what you felt. It is unlikely that any of us can remember the exact words of a conversation held even yesterday, much less ten, twenty years ago. But we remember the essence of it, and that is what we must convey to the reader. Your responsibility is to capture the essence of the interaction, to approximate the dialogue. There is no absolute truth. Toni Morrison said that 'it's not the difference between fact and fiction – it's the difference between fact and truth'."

Truth is what you observe and interpret through your observation.

Truth is your perception of fact.

The issue of libel and slander.

Basically, libel involves the publishing of a falsehood that harms someone.

In order to be sued for libel you must have (1) made a false, defamatory statement about (2) an identifiable person, that is (3) published and (4) causes injury to reputation.

As long as you stick to the truth and DON'T write things NOT already known about someone, which could be considered defamatory, you're fine. The ultimate in protection is, of course, a consent agreement. It doesn't help to change names. If a person is readily identifiable, it won't matter whether he is called Sylvester Rabbit or Bugs Bunny.

CHAPTER NINETEEN
ASSIGNMENTS FOR A 12-WEEK COURSE

Beginning IS half done.

From a mug given to me by my wife.

Lesson Number 1

Assignment: Write on 'A Turning Point In My Life' or on one of Dr. Phil's ten defining moments, seven critical choices or five pivotal people.

A turning point is most recognized in hindsight when we give credit to something we now realize changed our life, gave us focus or direction. They may be a good choice made when we encountered a 'fork in the road'. It may be an accomplishment or a person who provided guidance. We all have many turning points.

The following are suggestions:

Marriage

Your first job

A graduation

A hospitalization

Birth of a child

Moving to a new place (a new house)

An unexpected success

When you were fired from a job

Someone who has influenced your life or befriended you

Divorce

Military service

Time spent in prison

A financial setback

An accident

A change in careers

A job promotion or new assignment

Coming to USA

Remarriage

A school you attended

Death of a spouse or of a dear one

A special accomplishment

A crisis you had to overcome

A near-death experience

For those who are Dr. Phil watchers he has another approach to turning points. He actually categorizes them and states that we all have at least these twenty-two. The categories are: Your ten defining moments, your seven critical choices and your five pivotal people.

Your ten defining moments are those events in your life that shaped you. Our minds condense all of our experiences around those happenings that are most important.

Your seven critical choices are those crossroads that you have encountered in your life: what choices you made at each, why you made the particular choice you did, and what you think have been the results for your life.

Your five pivotal people may include your parents, spouse, or siblings. Pivotal people could include teachers, friends, and co-workers. Whoever these people are in your life, some of them are genuinely positive influences and some are horribly negative. Certain people do have a high impact on the formulation of your self-concept.

Lesson Number 2

Assignment: Write on 'Your Birth'

Memory sparklers:

What date was your birth?

Where were you born (city and state)?

In what hospital, home or taxi were you born?

If born at home what family members assisted?

Is there anything special about your birth? e.g. snow storm?

How was your name chosen?

Who was president when you were born?

Is there any historical time-in-place for your birth?

    - such as the year of the stock market crash, or five years before the passage of social security or the year Pearl Harbor was attacked.

Lesson Number 3

Assignment: Write on 'Your Elementary School Years' or
'Life With Your Nuclear Family'

Memory Sparklers:

Describe your family home.

Contrast your living conditions with present. Did you have a wood furnace, country living, family dog, out-door toilet?

If you didn't have television what was your entertainment?

Did you have siblings? Names? Did you get along with them?

How did you spend holidays?

What games did you play as a child?

Who were your friends?

What elementary school did you attend?

What was your most memorable experience?

What junior high or middle school did you attend?

Did you get into any mischief as a kid?

Who were your mentors as you grew up?

Were you a member of 4H, Cub Scouts, choir, etc.?

Did you have a paper route or farm chores?

What did these experiences mean to you?

Lesson Number 4

Assignment: Write on 'Your High School Years'

Memory Sparklers:

What high school did you attend?

Who were your close friends?

What clubs were you in?

Did you date?

What activities did you go to on dates?

What were your plans after high school graduation?

Did your family have expectations for you upon graduation?

Lesson Number 5

Assignment: Write on 'what you did immediately after high school'

Memory Sparklers:

The span of years following high school may be very different for many of you. It may have been spent in WWII or Korean War, in college, working the assembly line in a factory, working in the farming industry, etc. Your Life Chronology will dictate this to you.

How did you reach a decision to attend college?

What college?

Where did you stay?

How did you finance college?

Who were your roommates?

Describe your living arrangements?

What was your summer employment?

What did things cost at that time?

How did you satisfy your military obligation?

Lesson Number 6

Assignment: Write on 'Dating your future wife, first job, starting a family or choosing a career'.

Memory Sparklers:

When did you start dating?

How did you feel when you met Mr./Mrs. Right?

Or, why did you choose the single life?

Where, when, in what church were you married?

What kind of honeymoon?

Where did you live?

What was your first car?

What were the circumstances of your first Christmas together?

Do you have any humorous stories about your marriage?

first year together?

What was your first 'real' job?

How did you get it?

What was your pay?

What did your parents think about all this?

Lesson Number 7

Assignment: Write on the 'Family homestead' – that house your kids all call home; or the birth of a child.

Memory Sparklers:

Discuss where you settled down?

What was your family homestead?

Who were the key relatives that you interacted with?

What did you do with them?

What is the story behind the birth of each child?

Where were you living?

Did you stay with that first job or move around?

If you moved around what were the circumstances?

When, where, how much paid for your first house?

Any funny stories as the children grew?

How did you spend your vacations?

Discuss how holidays changed as you and your mate blended traditions and you became command post central for the holiday meals formerly hosted by family of origin.

Lesson Number 8

Assignment: Write about 'Your children's activities'

Memory Sparklers:

Were the children in Cub Scouts, 4H or other youth group?

In what way did you participate in their activities?

Did they have paper routes?

What were the family entertainment activities?

Were you a camping family?

Did you take family vacations?

Did you have any humorous stories about the family?

Any prom stories?

Were the kids in high school sports?

Were there any family deaths during this period?

What did this mean to you?

Lesson Number 9

Assignment: Write about 'Launching children'

Memory Sparklers:

What is the story about each child's high school graduation?

College graduation?
Marriage?

What type of job did your children work at upon being launched?

What did you and your spouse do for entertainment while the children were asserting their independence?

What were your hobbies and how did they change as you progressed through life?

Once the children were launched how did you feel?

Did you stay in the 'family homestead' or move?

Did you have pets as the children grew up?

Lesson Number 10

Assignment: Write about 'the empty nest period'.

Memory Sparklers:

Did you have any special wedding anniversaries?

How did you feel when the last child left the family?

What types of activities did you engage in with your adult children?

Were there any differences in how you and your spouse related after the children all left the home?

How did you fill your time after the children left?

Any additional or different hobbies?

Did you start taking 'couple' vacations?

Did you vacation with married children?

Identify your feelings when grandchildren started arriving?

Were you looking forward to retirement?

Lesson Number 11

Assignment: Write about 'Your retirement years'.

Memory Sparklers:

Were you looking forward to retirement?

Or were you retired as a by-product of illness, company downsizing or bankruptcy, spouse illness, etc.?

How did you handle retirement?

What replaced work in your life?

Did you travel, cruise, Elderhostel as part of retirement?

What were the circumstances of your move to Sun City Center?

Did you remain in your family 'homestead', move to a retirement facility in the same community or move to another location?

What was your relationship with children and grandchildren after retirement?

How did you feel about leaving the 'sandwich' generation?

Lesson Number 12

Assignment: During classtime be ready to tell the class how your memoirs are coming. I suggest that you ponder the following ten questions.

Overall organization of your memoirs:

1. Chapters with sidebars or
   Chapters subdivided in bites and episodes

2. How many chapters and how did you subdivide?

3. Percent completed?

4. Anticipated number of pages?

5. Photographs? How reproduced?

6. Published? What approach are you using?

7. Who do you anticipate giving copies to and how many copies would this be?

8. Any unique features?

9. What is your pattern for success?
   Write every day? What did you set aside (activities) to make room to write? Do you edit?

10. Is your family aware that you are doing this? If so, are they making suggestions? Or are they worried?

CHAPTER TWENTY
PUBLISHING AND PRESERVING PICTURES

Publishers are in business to make money, and if your books do well they don't care if you are male, female, or an elephant.

Margaret Atwood

As I said when you started this course I will tell you what I did, why I did it and how I did it. I now want to talk about how I published my first three books.

From Grandson To Grandfather

I'm writing about this book first since it is the one most of you are interested in. But remember that A Father's Story was my first book and this book was my publishing "teething ring".

My first job was to create my own publishing company and do it legally correct. Thus, since I did not desire to go into business, I did not create a 'company' or 'corporation'. So I cannot use the word 'company' or 'corporation' in my title.

I made application for the name 'Hans Hagar Press' through a process called 'fictitious name'. This way the State of Florida knows who is using the name and permits me to publish my books having a publishing name.

So I am my own publisher. What I cannot do myself I subcontracted to others. The printer was M and M Printing in Ruskin.

Here is a list of my expenses:

Library of Congress Control Number	$ 30.00
ISBN (10 numbers)	205.00
Fictitious Name	60.00
Bar Code for Cover	67.92
Printing Two Complete Copies at Staples	102.00
Typing the Manuscript	1200.00
Paper and Ribbons	50.00
Printing (500 copies)	<u>7652.42</u>
	$9367.37

Cost per copy = $18.73

The printing cost of $7,652.42 or $15.30 could have been reduced to about $7 per copy for 1500 copies. But I knew a personal memoir book --- unless you are rich or famous --- is not a best seller. I didn't think I could sell 500 copies let alone 1500. Even with the reduced cost per book the printing cost for 1500 would be $10,500 or almost another $3,000.00.

So why did I print 500 copies? I really wanted 100 copies for relatives and friends. The printer would print 100 using a different process --- yes, inferior but generally acceptable --- for about $5,000 or $50.00 per book. The non-printing cost of $1,714.95 would remain the same making the cost per book of $67.15. My thinking was if I could sell 200 copies of the 500 for $15 per book I would be money ahead and 200 copies to burn (Ha Ha).

At the cost of $506.93 I sent 800 solicitations to high school classmates, college classmates and retired faculty at the university. Only retired faculty seemed interested and I sold about 40, only recovering the cost of the mailing.

I suspended direct mailing. Friends purchased about forty and 87 have been gifts to relatives. The remaining are being used as a teaching textbook in memoir writing classes. Another twenty are set-aside for future relatives yet unborn. This verified what I knew before hand, unless you are rich or famous a personal memoirs book is not very marketable.

It was, however, the experience of a lifetime to be able to develop my writing hobby to the extent that I learn how to publish my own book at the grass roots level.

A Father's Story

This book was written as a grieving book and these details will be found on pages 364 to 366 in the From Grandson To Grandfather book.

At this time I knew two things. First, that I knew nothing about publishing a book and secondly, that I had a book which would sell nationally to people experiencing the trauma of a loved one dead or dying from AIDS.

I contracted with Fairway Press, the self-publishing division of CSS Publishing in Lima, Ohio. Thus I would have access to a publisher on a 'cafeteria' basis, that is, paying for each service that I needed.

By purchasing 1500 copies for $2400 and I had a $1350 start-up cost (typing, etc.) giving me a printing cost of $1.60 per book (1990 money) and start-up cost of $.90 per book for total cost of $2.50 per book. This is a 128-page book with only three pictures. It was the 187 pictures, 406 pages and printing only 500 copies, which ran up the printing cost of the memoirs book.

Fairway Press registered A Father's Story with the national book warehouser, Ingram's. Thus the book became available nation wide. Purchasing address labels resulted in a mailing to all infectious disease physicians, every Hospice in the nation and all community based AIDS support services in the country. About 8000 letters were sent resulting in 500 purchases. Another 500 were sold in bookstores. To date 1300 copies have been sold in every state in the union plus seven foreign countries.

Attached is the 1997 price list for Fairway Press. Remember prices go up about 10% per year.

FAIRWAY PRESS PRICES

Read down the left hand column to the number of pages your book will contain. Then read across to the number of books you want to order.

PAGES \ BOOKS	200	300	400	500	750	1000	1500	2000	2500	3000	4000	5000
42 to 70	5.46	4.25	3.40	2.88	2.20	1.85	1.50	1.32	1.22	1.16	1.06	1.01
71 to 80	6.42	4.61	3.70	3.15	2.43	2.06	1.69	1.49	1.39	1.32	1.22	1.17
81 to 90	6.89	4.96	4.00	3.42	2.65	2.26	1.87	1.67	1.56	1.49	1.38	1.32
91 to 100	7.35	5.32	4.31	3.69	2.88	2.47	2.06	1.85	1.73	1.65	1.54	1.48
101 to 110	7.81	5.68	4.61	3.96	3.11	2.68	2.24	2.03	1.89	1.81	1.70	1.64
111 to 120	8.28	6.03	4.91	4.23	3.33	2.88	2.43	2.20	2.06	1.98	1.86	1.79
121 to 130	8.74	6.39	5.21	4.50	3.56	3.09	2.61	2.38	2.23	2.14	2.02	1.95
131 to 140	9.16	6.71	5.47	4.73	3.74	3.25	2.75	2.51	2.35	2.26	2.13	2.06
141 to 150	9.58	7.01	5.73	4.95	3.93	3.41	2.89	2.64	2.48	2.38	2.25	2.17
151 to 160	9.99	7.32	5.98	5.18	4.11	3.57	3.03	2.77	2.60	2.49	2.36	2.28
161 to 170	10.41	7.63	6.24	5.40	4.29	3.73	3.17	2.89	2.72	2.61	2.47	2.39
171 to 180	10.83	7.94	6.50	5.63	4.47	3.89	3.31	3.02	2.84	2.73	2.58	2.50
181 to 190	11.25	8.25	6.76	5.85	4.66	4.06	3.45	3.15	2.97	2.85	2.70	2.61
191 to 200	11.66	8.56	7.01	6.08	4.84	4.22	3.59	3.28	3.09	2.96	2.81	2.71
201 to 210	12.08	8.87	7.27	6.30	5.02	4.38	3.73	3.41	3.21	3.08	2.92	2.82
211 to 220	12.50	9.18	7.53	6.53	5.20	4.54	3.87	3.54	3.33	3.20	3.03	2.93
221 to 230	12.92	9.49	7.79	6.75	5.39	4.70	4.01	3.66	3.46	3.32	3.15	3.04
231 to 240	13.33	9.80	8.04	6.98	5.57	4.86	4.15	3.79	3.58	3.43	3.26	3.15
241 to 250	13.75	10.11	8.30	7.20	5.75	5.02	4.29	3.92	3.70	3.55	3.37	3.26
251 to 260	14.17	10.42	8.56	7.43	5.93	5.18	4.43	4.05	3.82	3.67	3.49	3.37
261 to 270	14.59	10.74	8.82	7.65	6.12	5.35	4.57	4.18	3.95	3.79	3.60	3.48
271 to 280	15.01	11.05	9.08	7.88	6.30	5.57	4.71	4.31	4.07	3.91	3.71	3.60
281 to 290	15.43	11.36	9.33	8.11	6.49	5.67	4.85	4.44	4.20	4.03	3.83	3.71
290 to 300	15.85	11.67	9.59	8.34	6.67	5.83	4.99	4.57	4.32	4.15	3.94	3.82
301 to 310	16.27	11.98	9.85	8.56	6.85	5.99	5.14	4.70	4.44	4.27	4.06	3.93
311 to 320	16.69	12.30	10.11	8.79	7.04	6.16	5.28	4.83	4.57	4.39	4.17	4.04
321 to 330	17.10	12.61	10.37	9.02	7.22	6.32	5.42	4.96	4.69	4.51	4.29	4.15
331 to 340	17.52	12.92	10.63	9.24	7.41	6.48	5.56	5.09	4.82	4.63	4.40	4.26
341 to 350	17.94	13.23	10.89	9.47	7.59	6.64	5.70	5.22	4.94	4.75	4.52	4.38
351 to 360	18.36	13.55	11.14	9.70	7.77	6.81	5.84	5.35	5.06	4.87	4.63	4.49
361 to 370	18.78	13.86	11.40	9.92	7.96	6.97	5.98	5.48	5.19	4.99	4.75	4.60
371 to 380	19.20	14.17	11.66	10.15	8.14	7.13	6.12	5.61	5.31	5.11	4.86	4.71

INCLUDES

Editing, Typesetting, & Proofreading from original manuscript

Note: Fairway Press provides a quoted price based on the individual specifications of each job. Prices listed are "per book" prices. Prices are subject to change.

Prices listed include printing of 5 1/4" X 8 1/4" pages on 60# white paper and printing and binding of laminated cover on white 10 point coated one side cover stock. Prices also include 1 proof copy of text, 1 cover ___, 1 cover negatives, and ink.

Prices
Effective 1/97

CAMERA READY PRICES

Read down the left hand column to the number of pages your book will contain. Then read across to the number of books you want to order.

PAGES \ BOOKS	200	300	400	500	750	1000	1500	2000	2500	3000	4000	5000
42 to 70	3.72	2.76	2.28	1.99	1.60	1.40	1.20	1.10	1.04	1.01	.95	.92
71 to 80	3.87	2.90	2.42	2.13	1.74	1.54	1.34	1.24	1.18	1.15	1.09	1.06
81 to 90	4.01	3.05	2.56	2.27	1.88	1.69	1.49	1.39	1.33	1.29	1.24	1.21
91 to 100	4.16	3.19	2.71	2.42	2.03	1.83	1.63	1.53	1.47	1.44	1.38	1.35
101 to 110	4.30	3.33	2.85	2.56	2.17	1.97	1.77	1.67	1.61	1.58	1.52	1.49
111 to 120	4.45	3.48	2.99	2.70	2.31	2.12	1.92	1.82	1.76	1.72	1.67	1.64
121 to 130	4.59	3.62	3.13	2.84	2.45	2.26	2.06	1.96	1.90	1.86	1.81	1.78
131 to 140	4.69	3.72	3.23	2.94	2.55	2.36	2.16	2.06	2.00	1.96	1.91	1.88
141 to 150	4.79	3.82	3.33	3.04	2.65	2.45	2.25	2.15	2.09	2.05	2.00	1.97
151 to 160	4.89	3.91	3.43	3.13	2.74	2.55	2.35	2.25	2.19	2.15	2.10	2.07
161 to 170	4.98	4.01	3.52	3.23	2.84	2.65	2.45	2.35	2.29	2.25	2.20	2.17
171 to 180	5.08	4.11	3.62	3.33	2.94	2.74	2.54	2.44	2.38	2.34	2.29	2.26
181 to 190	5.18	4.21	3.72	3.43	3.04	2.84	2.64	2.54	2.48	2.44	2.39	2.36
191 to 200	5.28	4.30	3.82	3.52	3.13	2.94	2.74	2.64	2.58	2.54	2.49	2.46
201 to 210	5.38	4.40	3.92	3.62	3.23	3.03	2.83	2.73	2.67	2.63	2.58	2.55
211 to 220	5.48	4.50	4.02	3.72	3.33	3.13	2.93	2.83	2.77	2.73	2.68	2.65
221 to 230	5.57	4.60	4.11	3.82	3.43	3.23	3.03	2.93	2.87	2.83	2.78	2.75
231 to 240	5.67	4.69	4.21	3.91	3.52	3.32	3.12	3.02	2.96	2.92	2.87	2.84
241 to 250	5.77	4.79	4.31	4.01	3.62	3.42	3.22	3.12	3.06	3.02	2.97	2.94
251 to 260	5.87	4.89	4.41	4.11	3.72	3.52	3.32	3.22	3.16	3.12	3.07	3.04
261 to 270	5.97	4.99	4.51	4.21	3.82	3.62	3.42	3.32	3.26	3.22	3.17	3.14
271 to 280	6.07	5.09	4.61	4.31	3.92	3.72	3.52	3.42	3.36	3.32	3.27	3.24
281 to 290	6.17	5.19	4.71	4.41	4.01	3.81	3.61	3.51	3.45	3.41	3.36	3.33
290 to 300	6.27	5.29	4.80	4.51	4.11	3.91	3.71	3.61	3.55	3.51	3.46	3.43
301 to 310	6.37	5.39	4.90	4.61	4.21	4.01	3.81	3.71	3.65	3.61	3.56	3.53
311 to 320	6.47	5.49	5.00	4.71	4.31	4.11	3.91	3.87	3.75	3.71	3.66	3.63
321 to 330	6.56	5.58	5.10	4.80	4.41	4.21	4.01	3.91	3.85	3.81	3.76	3.73
331 to 340	6.66	5.68	5.20	4.90	4.51	4.31	4.11	4.01	3.95	3.91	3.86	3.83
341 to 350	6.76	5.78	5.30	5.00	4.61	4.40	4.21	4.11	4.05	4.00	3.96	3.93
351 to 360	6.86	5.88	5.39	5.10	4.70	4.50	4.30	4.20	4.14	4.10	4.05	4.02
361 to 370	6.96	5.98	5.49	5.20	4.80	4.60	4.40	4.30	4.24	4.20	4.15	4.12
371 to 380	7.06	6.08	5.59	5.30	4.90	4.70	4.50	4.40	4.34	4.30	4.25	4.22

CAMERA READY

camera ready—the pages are already set in type and do not require any additional typesetting or alterations. What you send us is what your printed pages will look like.

Note: Express Press provides a quoted price based on the individual specifications of each job. Prices listed are "per book" prices. Prices are subject to change.

Prices listed include printing of 5 1/4" X 8 1/4" pages on 60# white paper and printing and binding of laminated cover on white 10 point coated one side cover stock. Prices also include 1 proof copy of text, 1 cover proof, cover negatives, and ink.

Prices
Effective 1/97

Grin And Share It

This is my wife's memoirs. The 173-page memoir contains a narrative section of 145 pages. She has made ten copies for selected family members.

In the back of each book will be found 27 pages of pictures. These are all 8-1/2" by 11" sheets of photographic paper. As many as six pictures appear on each page. These are perfect – sometimes even better – photographic reproductions of the original. The cost was $2 per page and using regular paper the cost drops to $1.39. We used Kinko's in Brandon, which has excellent copy machines.

The per copy price of her memories is:

27 sheets of pictures @ $2 per	$ 54.00
173 sheets of paper duplicated @ $.07	12.11
106 plastic sheet holders @ $.075	6.30
1 three ring binder @ $7 per	7.00
typing ($400 total) – for ten copies @	40.00
	$121.06

The $.07 per sheet price is from Staples in Brandon and based on a volume business of 1000 sheets or more. Those fluent with computers can eliminate the typing expense.

Quick mathematics will tell you that it cost us $1,210.60 for ten copies. This process is probably reflective of what most students in my classes employ --- doing everything themselves and making only enough copies for special relatives.

Personal Computer Generated Copy and Pictures

As you all know computers and I haven't bonded. I usually talk only about the technology I use. Because of this I try to find a computer geek to give a talk in class about opscanning pictures into the computer for computer generated copy.

M and M Printing of Ruskin did the printing for my memoirs. All of my work was on CDs and downloaded into their computer. My 187 pictures were numbered and keyed to the captions that were on a separate CD. The operator had to opscan each picture into the computer and number them. I then sat on my stool behind her giving directions.

Starting with the first picture and going in sequence my directions were:

1. The page it is to appear on.

2. Where on the page? Top, bottom, middle and side.

3. Cropping to done – want to eliminate someone?

4. Outline, e.g., oval, square, rectangular – in what direction?

5. Then bringing the caption onto this page.

6. The type of wrap around. Please examine my memoirs for examples of how the captions were wrapped around the picture.

After each picture and caption was added the subsequent page numbering changed thus the importance of starting with the first picture and continuing in order. This expanded the book from about 300 pages of narrative to its current 406. It was fascinating to watch and to be in control of the decision making process while the computer operator pressed buttons and dragged with the mouse.

Clearly, with 187 pictures and captions, this was a slow process and took days to complete. It was very labor intense which contributed greatly to the cost of the printing price. Examining my wife's memoirs, you will find that the pictures represent 76% of the cost.

For those of you who are computer savvy this provides an option you may want to pursue. If not perhaps you have a friend who, for a price, will make computer generated pictures an option for your memoirs.

FROM GRANDSON TO GRANDFATHER

Reflections of a University Professor on his Career and Family

EDMUND HANSEN

Key Topics in this book about Edmund Hansen

1. His peaks and valleys experienced living life.

2. The changing life "hats" from son and grandson, giving way to husband and father and, finally, grandfather.

3. His role as sweetheart, lover and husband to the same woman for forty-five years (as of 2001).

4. The antidotal humorous stories told about raising four sons.

5. His insightful perspective as a faculty member living through forty years of the history of the University of Wisconsin - Oshkosh as it went from a teachers college of 500 students to a regional university encompassing four undergraduate colleges with 12,000 students.

6. His candid portrayal of the individuals employed at the university in key positions as the school went through the civil rights riots of the 60's, the financial crises which precipitated the tremendous changes of the 70's, and its emergence as a school of academic excellence, i.e., its Golden Age, in the 80's.

Key Writing Features in this book by Edmund Hansen

1. Family stories are told in episode format. An episode, like family camping, is told in its entirety and not integrated piece-meal chronologically with other on-going activities.

2. Career periods are told intact in separate chapters and not integrated with family activities. This allows the reader to separate the family man from the university professor.

ISBN 0-9709943408

51495

9780970943408

FIRST EDITION
Copyright 2001 by
Edmund Hansen

PUBLISHED BY
Hans Hagar Press
Sun City Center, FL 33573

Library of Congress Control Number: 2001131895
ISBN 0-9709434-0-7

Other books by author:
A Father's Story: The Story of a Son's Battle with AIDS
Fairway Press
ISBN 0-7880-0663-0
Distributed by Ingrams Book Company
Copyright: 1996

Printed in U.S.A.

2

FROM GRANDSON TO GRANDFATHER

REFLECTIONS OF A UNIVERSITY PROFESSOR ON HIS CAREER AND FAMILY

BY: EDMUND HANSEN

HANS HAGAR PRESS
SUN CITY CENTER, FLORIDA

132

Acknowledgements

The task of writing these memoirs was started following our Amazon cruise in February of 1999. Writing the narrative took until the summer of 2000 to complete.

Sorting through thirty volumes of family photo albums, selecting the most representative one hundred-seventy pictures and writing the captions consumed most of the 2000 summer. Some pictures in chapter two were borrowed from Hugh Corbett.

I never learned to type and even if I did, computers and I are not compatible. My wife, Ginny, did all the typing. Also Ginny and her computer did the script editing.

Ginny is also responsible for providing additional advisory help. Whenever my memory was fuzzy or my writing insensitive to another's feelings, she was there to talk things out. Our sharing made the writing very enjoyable.

Thank you, Ginny, for your many contributions.

Dedication

This book is dedicated to all my relatives everywhere but especially:

My grandparents:
Charles and Bertha Damsheuser, Hans and Sophia Hansen.
My parents: Harvey and Florence Hansen.
My wife: Virginia (Ginny) Hansen
Our sons: Lee, Scott, Dean and Perry Hansen
Our daughters-in-law: Julia, Robin and Kelley Hansen
Our grandchildren: Eric, Ben, Kymberly, Nicole, Melanie and Jon

My brother: James Hansen
My brother in law: Robert Krull
My sisters-in-law: Myrt Gracey, Virginia Hansen and Mary Krull-Greenlee

My nephews and nieces: Brian and Michael Hansen, Cheryl Constantine and Tina Jeffers

My cousins everywhere:

To our Asian side of the family: These are our loved ones who came from Southeast Asia with the names of Luangpraseuth and Chomsisengphet. This book is also dedicated to them, their descendents and those grafted into our family through marriage.

Introduction

From *Grandson to Grandfather* depicts the changing roles each of us play while traversing through life. And it brings home two old adages: 'Life is not a bowl of cherries' and 'Life is what you make of it'; that all individuals have adversity and we are contributors to writing the script of the role each play on the stage of life.

The book begins with my birth and includes my role on life's stage as: grandson; son; brother; the many faceted relationship of sweetheart, lover and husband; father to four sons; grandfather to six and 'father and grandfather" to an ever increasing number of our Asian family. The humorous antidotes, life's activities, relationships with family and friends, and the inevitable death of family members are all here.

Family love and commitment was a unifying thread as I traversed life. Contained within this book is my perspective on the love and commitment shown by those who cared for me and, hopefully, how I learned and passed this on to others as I became responsible for their care and well being.

Concerning the inevitable death of loved ones and other adversities, remember that the pleasures and successes of life are nice but character is hewn out of the adversities. It is not until I walked through the fires of life did I know what metal I was made of. Any memoir on only the 'good stuff' is simply self promoting. It is necessary to disclose and discuss how I dealt with the 'hard stuff"; how I, with the support of others, picked myself up and moved on. All this will be found within the covers of this book. But there is more.

Men of my generation lived two lives: the family man and the career or working man. Any memoir of me would be incomplete if my career and its' achievements plus trials and tribulations were not included. This was a large part of my life and to know me, in addition to knowing the family man, is to understand my relationship to work. Work was how I contributed to society and how I earned the money to feed my family.

I realize not everyone is interested in both facets of my dual life. Those chapters which are career exclusively have a 'C' after

the chapter number. For those who want just the family man, the 'C' chapters could be skipped without losing continuity of the family man.

While writing family activities I did my best to imbed them in the culture and mores' in which they occurred. The reader must be able to place himself in the culture of the day to appreciate my life's excitement.

By writing in episode format an activity or interest is written up completely and may, like the camping episode, cut across several years. Because of this, information which impacts several episodes is repeated but usually with a different emphasis.

The 160 episodes are identified on the 'CONTENTS' page. This will aid in quickly identifying information desired and how to find information already read.

A brief summary of chapters for the family man follows:

1. Growing up: 1936 to 1951 (my age 0 to 15)
2. Teenage years: 1951 to 1954 (my age 15 to 18)
3. Attending College and Marriage: 1954 to 1958 (my age 18 to 22)
4. Early Family and Career: 1958 to 1963 (my age 22 to 27)
5. First Two Years of College Teaching: 1963 to 1965 (my age 27 to 29)
10. The Family of Six Settles Down and Matures: 1966 to 1977 (my age 30 to 41)
14. Launching Children: 1975 to 1987 (my age 39 to 51)
15. Leaving the Family Homestead: 1986 (my age 50)
18. Adult Children, Grandkids and Death of a Son: 1987 to 1994 (my age 51 to 58)
20. Adjusting to Life Without Work and Physically Disabled
21. The Retired Life (my age 57 and beyond)
    A capsulated list of my career chapters are:
6. Career Stalled and Professional Implications: 1966
7. Overcoming Adversity and Moving On: 1966 to 1972
8. The Turbulent 60's and Black Thursday
9. The Arrival of Chancellor Birnbaum and New Turmoil: 1973
11. New Career Directions: 1975 to 1981
12. Opportunity, Bureaucratic Intrigue and Biding Time: 1982 to 1987

Lastly, everyone wants to leave a legacy for those who come in succeeding generations. I have always held books in high esteem. It is only fitting that, in addition to having touched lives, that I leave not wealth, jewels or artifacts but a book for those who want to know my circumstances on the life path I took. Put in another context, to see the life cards I was dealt and understand my decisions in contributing to the script for playing these cards on the stage of life.

To my sons I want this book to be a record which is as complete and as accurate as possible of our togetherness. I also want this book to be a memorial to those relatives and friends who contributed to me becoming the person I am. I, like you my sons, did not mature in a vacuum but was guided and socialized by preceding relatives and those people place around me.

For my grandchildren who now live fifteen hundred miles away, meet Grandpa through his writing. You were too young to ask me about my life before I retired to Florida. And your time visiting us in Florida has been very limited and spent doing fun things.

A final comment about the book is necessary. Remember that this book is a memoir. I am writing the events as I remember them. Some comments, especially about professional colleagues, are very candid. No malice or slander was intended by using your names while I attempted to portray as accurately as I recall the historical events. Three students names are fictitious. These are Ellington Anonymous, Gerry Nothisname and Chang. Student confidentiality and common sense requires this. Likewise the name Father Good Friend is fictitious.

Remember that everyone sees and interprets life through the 'rose colored glasses' of our own experiences. That these memoirs were written many years after the event is another consideration. But everything written is as accurate as I remember it.

Please understand that this book is intended to provide the bits of glass in the kaleidoscope of my life. Enjoy.

Edmund Hansen

CONTENTS

(Chapters and Episodes within Chapters)

11

12

137

CHAPTER 1
Launched and Named

"What is the sex, Doctor? I need to know". My mother was awakening from the anesthetic. Father was holding her hand.

"Well, Mr. and Mrs. Hansen" Dr. Swanton said, "You have another boy". That's the way it went, they tell me. I was born on a Tuesday March 9th, 1936 in Appleton, Wisconsin at St. Elizabeth Hospital.

Sure my parents were happy to have a healthy and normal child. But being second born, mother clearly wanted a girl. She even had the name Juanita picked out for me. That's enough to scare anyone into becoming a boy.

Father wouldn't get involved picking out girl names. But now, since I wasn't a girl he had a renewed interest in name selection.

"I think naming him after my father would be a great honor. Let's name him Hans", was Father's suggestion. Mother responded, "Oh, no. I don't want any 'ole country' name".

They thought about it for a while and finally settled on Edmund. This was the name of the male actor in a moving picture show they had just seen. So, they thought, I was launched with an American name.

At least that's what they thought. In December of 1997 I received a letter from one Anne-Karin Aarvik of Trondheim, Norway. Her uncle, she explained, was Edmund Hansen and he had a son Edmund. The latter was born in 1950 shortly after her uncle immigrated to the US. Two days after the birth, her uncle was killed and she lost contact with the wife. Anna was searching for her cousin and writing to all 12 Edmund Hansens' found on the Internet. Was I he? She wrote.

It appears that after all the effort of my mother; I apparently have an 'ole country' name after all. Poor mother, she tried.

Probably when I was born I was slapped on my bare behind like all other babies. But I don't remember that. And I was, according to my mother, breast-fed like most babies of the day. But I can't remember that either. I'm sure my mother appreciated this.

My parents talked about how bad the winter was when I was born. They showed me many pictures of snowdrifts and high piles of snow formed when shoveling.

Father's car was taken out of storage only 10 days before my birth. The car was stored each winter, raised on blocks to preserve the tires. The city didn't have the equipment to keep the streets clear of snow.

The only house I remember prior to starting kindergarten was a cream-colored colonial style house on Summer Street. A detached single car garage was in back where my father kept his car, an Essex.

The back yard contained a generous garden with a cherry tree. My mother would fight the robins every summer to see who got the most cherries.

The neighbors had a daughter in high school and she became our babysitter. Each morning after we had the sitter, mother would make buttermilk pancakes. That was our treat for being good.

The "we" at that time included my one sibling, Jim, who was two and one-half years older.

When I was five we moved across town to 826 West Third Street. I lived here until I left the family to attend college. This is the house I remember well and always call The Family Homestead.

This is one of just a few pictures of me as a baby. I'm probably under one year old which dates the picture to the summer of 1936.

Notice that Jim and I were dressed in matching shirts. I'll guess my age as 3 so the picture was taken the summer of 1939. Mother has slimmed down since the previous picture.

Christmases

Memories of childhood always seemed to settle on holidays and what was done to change the routine of daily living. My parents always went to church on Christmas Eve. Christmas Eve was also the children's program. I was shy and didn't care for public speaking, so I usually became a shepherd.

After the Christmas program, as we were exiting church, we would receive a bag of "goodies". The standard fare was an apple, a candy bar, several pieces of hard candy and a lot of peanuts (in the shell) for filler. The minister would end the service by saying, "Now go home with your family and see what Santa Claus brought".

Every year on the way home from church on Christmas Eve, Mother would rant and rave, saying, "When will he realize that Santa Claus comes when we're sleeping and not before?" She always wanted to open presents on Christmas morning and not try to put two hyper boys to bed after opening presents containing toys. As Jim, my big brother, and I got older, we just "humored" Mother with such comments as, "Oh really!" or "Some people never learn."

Christmas morning was spent opening presents and eating stollen. Noon was always a big meal—goose when Grandpa lived with us, and turkey after Grandpa passed on. We always had tons of candy and cookies. Mother hand dipped her own chocolates and we would have caramels, double chocolates, toffee, chocolate covered peanut brittle, cream centers, peanut clusters and mints. The cookies were the traditional Christmas kind and were trimmed with colored sugars.

I Remember World War II Well.

A lot of my childhood memories centered on World War II. I was five in December 1941 at its beginning and nine when it ended in August 1945. The following article was written for The Tampa Tribune to capture some of these memories.

The night was dark with clouds obscuring the stars and moon. I sat in the dark living room with my parents and older brother staring out the windows at the shadows made by shining streetlights. Our game was to see who would be the first to see the helmeted air raid warden looking for blackout non-compliance.

It was 1943 and I was seven years old. While we were one thousand miles from the Atlantic coast, yet here in Appleton, Wisconsin, we were engaged in an air raid practice drill.

I have great admiration for the men and women of our country who fought World War II and sympathy for those, on either side, who experienced the air raids, which I only practiced. Yet, though living out of harms way, our life still centered on the conflict.

When Japan bombed Pearl Harbor on December 7th, 1941, my father went throughout the house breaking every piece of China that said, 'Made in Japan'. Germans settled our area of Wisconsin and my German born maternal grandfather lived with us. Thus our German beer steins were spared his anger.

Food was either scarce or rationed. Meat was the item rationed. I spent a lot of time on my bicycle making the rounds of the small neighborhood grocery stores trying to purchase potatoes and cooking oil. Even butter was not available. It was impossible to buy chocolate.

But living in Wisconsin meant milk was always available and in quantity. The milk we purchased was not homogenized so the fat particles collected and floated to the top. We would pour this off and collect it in a gallon glass jug. It was my job to shake this cream until it coagulated. The glob so formed was butter. Salt was added to the butter to preserve it. The liquid remaining, buttermilk, was used for pancakes.

Then came gasoline rationing. Father worked for the local Electric Company and was required to travel in his car to its various substations. Because of his need to travel additional gas coupons were issued to him.

The restricted use of gasoline was necessary because of the military need. People learned to car pool, take the bus or walk.

Local gasoline stations suffered financially with reduced business. With father's extra gas need he was able to work out an arrangement with a local gasoline station. He gave the station all his business in exchange for their reserving and storing a set of tires to be purchased at a later date. Tires were also in short supply. New cars were not available during the war years. All vehicle production was for the military. A second national benefit of gas rationing was it meant auto conservation. People simple couldn't do any leisure driving or travel great distances for vacations. Cars would have to last for the duration of the war. Only a limited number of used cars became available for purchase.

Everyone was expected to recycle tin cans and toothpaste tubes. The latter would not meet current health standards since they were made out of lead.

Few people needed convincing of the need to recycle. We all knew of the German U-boat menace in the North Atlantic and Gulf of Mexico.

After the war we learned the magnitude of the menace. U-boats sank two hundred US ships in our territorial waters in 1942 and 1943.

What we did know was that shipping was done at a price. To waste or not recycle would require additional shipping and this could mean the life of a seaman.

I was in elementary school during the war. As kids we saved our dimes and quarters to buy war bond stamps for our war bond books. After we saved $18.75 we would receive a $25 war bond. The fact that we purchased stamps rather than save money meant the military had immediate use of our money.

When our school saved enough to buy a Jeep the army sent soldiers to show us a vehicle like the one we just purchased. I can still see that Jeep going up and down the outside steps to our school.

We kids mobbed soldiers, sailors or airmen returning home on furlough. We all wanted our picture taken with them. Of course the school principal would have them talk to us at a general assembly.

Our family always listened to the national news in the evening. I still hear the drone of newscasters talking about the war. One I especially remember is a man by the name of Gabriel Heater. He was my father's favorite.

As kids we idealized military men and the war. It was "us" against "them" on a national scale. Yet, even as kids the stars hanging in everyone's window were a grim reminder of the ugliness of what was going on. A Gold star, Silver star and Blue star stood for a loved one dead, wounded, or serving.

Finally the war was over. I went down town with my buddy and his father. Department stores on the main street were pumping confetti out their top windows. Soon the street was covered like wintertime snow. We kids began sweeping it up and "recycling" by throwing confetti into open car windows. No one really cared. It was just one big celebration.

So did my father's 1938 Buick make it through the war? Yes it did. In fact, it lasted until 1949 when his name came to the top of the wait list for a new car.

My Brother

I had just one sibling, a brother Jim, two years and five months older. Jim was three years ahead of me in school.

Jim and I were very different from each other. I was totally perturbed with my parents for not recognizing our differences. Jim was older and went through school experiences before me. Jim was a good student. I always heard, "Why can't you do as well as Jim? You've got the same parents." As I got older, I silently rebelled by not studying. My grades showed it. It wasn't until I was a senior in high school that I realized I was only hurting myself. I went all out that year in senior physics and got a better grade than Jim three years earlier. The monkey was off my back. But our relationship suffered because I viewed Jim as the "enemy". Only deliberate effort and discussions changed this attitude with Jim when I was about 40 years of age.

Jim and I had another major difference. He was very "adventurous" (our parents had a different adjective for this trait) while I was more docile. Even to this day, Jim and I have many talks about this aspect of our upbringing. It was always a "ghost" in our relationship and affected our relating as adults.

Our parents were very conservative people, the-salt-of-the-earth, who continued in many of the "old country" ways. But Jim was always testing the boundaries. Certainly a parent must establish boundaries for their child; they must, however, expand these boundaries throughout the child's early years, whenever the child is able to assume more responsibility for himself. These boundaries never expanded rapidly enough for Jim. He was always "rattling" his cage. He was forever on our father's s— list.

And what was I doing when Jim was getting his "reaming out"? Watching, listening, and learning where the boundaries were so I

tremendous contribution to the person I would become. He also provided the example of the type of loyal employee portrayed in his philosophy (next chapter).

The way Mr. Close assumed leadership he would provide an example I would emulate for the rest of my life. Because of his example I was able to assume the position of Cubmaster when my sons joined Cub Scouts. I had a great desire to be the example of leadership for my sons that Mr. Close was for me.

I Remember My Paper Route Well

The third adult male who contributed greatly to my growing up was Father. It was stressed to both Jim and I that at the age of twelve we would have paper routes. No choice. But we wouldn't be alone.

Yes, I remember it well. Especially the winters.

The following article written for the Tampa Tribune was published December 1, 1998.

At the age of twelve I inherited Jim's paper route. That was an experience. In the winter, I would leave my home about 3:30 in the afternoon. The walk down Third Street to Memorial Drive, about one and one-half blocks, was easy. After all I had just left home.

Turning right onto Memorial Drive put me on course for crossing the Memorial Bridge—so named in memory of those who died in the war-to-end-all-wars.

Again it was only one and one-half blocks to the bridge. But the bridge was three blocks long. Now was the time to make sure all parts of my body were covered. It would be hard adjusting my clothing without the protection of houses.

My load of one hundred fifty-one newspapers filled the two carrier bags. They were slung over my head on either side of my shoulders. The weight now transferred to my back allowed my arms to dangle free permitting my hands to keep the bags in place. This prevented them from working around in front of me hitting my legs as I walked.

Residents of the northland quickly learn the ways of the harsh winters. In November the snows come and accumulate on the frozen tundra—so named because the water in the earth freezes mak-

ing the ground feel and act like ice.

Snowplows push the snow into large ridges along the streets narrowing them and reducing the number of traffic lanes. Bicycles must now be stored until April.

If the day is warm—above 0 degrees Fahrenheit—walking on snow and compressing it gives a sound like walking on cardboard. But if the day is cold then a loud crunching sound is heard as hundreds of frozen snow crystals are broken simultaneously. The sound heard indicates the outside temperature.

Snow never seemed cold when it landed on my face. But if the wind is blowing the hand knit facemask lovingly knit by my mother must be worn. With a cold temperature and wind the "wind-chill temperature" could be minus fifty or worse.

Crossing the Memorial Bridge was always a challenge. The bridge spanned the Fox River from very high embankments. The center of the bridge was even higher to permit river traffic to pass under it. This being possible only in warm weather months since the river freezes over in December. The bridge ran north and south with a sidewalk on the eastern side fully exposed to the wind. I would be walking from north to south to get to my paper route.

The prevailing westerly winds cause me to face east while I walked south. This was great. For far beneath me and perhaps one mile away was the local Power Company. It once used the river to generate hydroelectricity but increased demand for electricity from urban growth forced a change to coal for power. Because of this large quantities of coal were consumed all of which had to be brought in by barges in the summer months. Now, in the winter months, gigantic piles of coal were visible from the bridge. Also visible was the physical structure of the plant. It was upon this structure that a large sign was constructed.

Evening comes early in the northland. As I walked the bridge with the sun sinking in the west the colorful lights of the sign were made even more visible. The sign contained thousands of electric light bulbs arranged to communicate a message, which said: PEACE ON EARTH GOOD WILL TO MEN.

The message was warming and also was the realization that my father worked in the plant. At 5PM, when work ended, I knew he would come with the family car in search of me. With this mes-

Father and his brothers all had paper routes since the age of ten. His sisters cleaned houses and did washing. The money was needed by the family for daily living.

Our family didn't need my route money for daily living but Father felt, in addition to earning money for college, the paper route was a teaching ground for lessons needed for life. These included: a work ethic, to learn to serve rather than be served, how to meet the public and even be courteous under adverse conditions, how to save and spend money and how to complete an assigned task even if you didn't feel like it. Father was right. I always felt I had the advantage over those who didn't learn to work when young.

The paper route was a family project and Mother helped in other ways. During the summer months she would help me fold the papers. We had no rubber bands or plastic sleeves in those days. Carefully folded papers could be thrown great distances without opening up. These papers were delivered while riding my mono speed balloon tires bike—my first business expense was purchasing this bike—throwing each customer's paper onto his front porch.

Each Saturday morning was spent collecting money from customers. When I returned home Mother would count the money and record amounts in a ledger book. At noon Father drove me to the newspaper office to pay my weekly bill. The money remaining was my salary. When $18.75 of salary had accumulated Father would buy a $25 US Savings Bond in my name. Any tips received were my spending money.

My four years as a newspaper carrier are remembered well. Both the hardships and the warmth of family working together. Father set the stage for me to become the responsible citizen I am today.

While I could only spend the tips don't think I didn't have plenty of money. My paper route was in a very affluent neighborhood and Father saw to it that I did a very good job. The customers generously rewarded my efforts.

Most of my money was spent on my hobby, photography. I purchased a 35mm camera plus all accessories, projector for slide showing, and a dark room for developing film and printing pictures. I self taught myself how to use all the equipment.

sage and my father's immediate application I knew I wasn't alone.

Once my father found me the remaining papers were placed in the car and passed out the window on an as needed basis. My father was fulfilling his promise made to me, that being, "I can't afford to finance your college education but Mother and I will help YOU earn the money."

My father was one of eleven children of immigrant Danish parents. He was forced to quit high school when his father died while all older brothers were in France fighting WWI. He was determined I would have the educational opportunities he didn't.

I had a paper route for four years. My work ethic, devotion to completing a job and ability to get along with people were learned at this early age. And trusty Elmer was always waiting when I got home. I'm in 8th or 9th grade in the picture so the date is either 1950 or 1951. Notice the clothes drying behind me. Electric clothes dryers were yet to be invented.

I didn't have any other vices. Dating wasn't started until age sixteen. This is dealt with in the next chapter.

Broken Arm

Don't think for a minute that life was all roses. No, like everybody else, I had my heartache. When I was in 7th grade, I broke my arm, just above the wrist, playing football with my friends. By the time I went home, one of the bones was noticeably sagging lower than the other. It was obviously broken. Father took me to the family doctor that same evening (it was Sunday).

I'm appalled thinking back at the medical care of the day. I was placed sitting in a rocking chair; Father held my upper arm against the chair while the doctor pulled my hand until my green stick fracture "popped" in place—all without anesthetic. What PAIN!!!! I haven't liked doctors ever since. I spent six weeks with my arm in a cast writing left-handed. I'm fearful of pain to this day.

Grandpa's Death

Death is part of life. Yet the first death experienced is traumatic. And it always is for the death of a loved one. When both happen together the impact can be catastrophic.

Grandpa became sick. Not seriously sick, but sick. He could still take most of his meals with us downstairs. One morning, after he was sick two weeks, I was sent upstairs to get Grandpa for breakfast.

After knocking, I entered the room. He was already sitting in bed and staring out the window. I walked in and positioned myself between him and the window. That's when I saw the gun and knew he was dead. I ran from the room, never to see him again.

As I think back unto this time of my life. I had several questions that needed answering. We didn't talk about feelings in my family so only time and experience would provide the answers. These questions included: Didn't Grandpa know he was my ideal person and that I still needed him? Didn't he know that I loved him and that his suicide would hurt me? Is Grandpa in heaven or, because of the suicide, hell?

My reasoning went further. If Grandpa did it then it must be OK. So when one is tired of living one simply shoots himself. I

wondered how old one should be before buying the gun? That's so one is ready for that time in life. It would take decades before I would realize suicide was an inappropriate solution to a problem.

We often must live with experiences that are not of our choosing. I believe we can all identify "pits" in our lives or times we were swept away in a life "avalanche". In most cases we have to choose to walk away from the situation, seek help or stay stuck, perhaps for life.

Unfortunately I chose to bury much of what happened in my sub-consciousness. Part of my emotional development became arrested or "stuck" at the age of ten. So much of myself was invested in Grandpa that my self worth and ability to love would take a long time to recover.

It would be forty years before I could verbalize what happened that day. He meant so much to me.

This picture was taken between 1921 and 1923. Shown here are L - R: Mother, Uncle Carl who four years older than mother and my Damsheuser grandparents. Mother is between 13 and 15 years of age. They were living on the five acre farm at this time.

Wayne made an imposing figure as he looked down at Hugh from his 6 foot 4 inch frame. Clearly you would want to be friends with Wayne and not cross him nor have him tackle you in a football game.

As we left Wayne shook Hugh's hand. It took Hugh the next ten minutes to straighten out his fingers.

Hugh never said another word about playing football.

Father's Philosophy

It is so easy to criticize and say, "But I don't have this" or "I didn't have that" or "If only——". I want to go on record as thankful for the family, the circumstances, the period of time and the country I was born into. I had no hand in choosing these. But I am happy with the choices made for me.

After all, I could have been born in a country that wouldn't allow class mobility, or born to a family with no ambition, or born Black or Native American. Please, this is not a racial statement but a realization that Whites in the US have had advantages not available to Blacks or to Native Americans, or those born in poverty regardless of race.

Forest Gump's philosophical statement on life is, "Life is like a box of chocolates. You never know what you're going to get." This certainly fits my last two paragraphs. But, to carry this further, I got some choice pieces.

Ed Hansen's version of Gump's philosophy is, "Life is like a hand in a card game. You have no choice in what cards are dealt. But I have a hell-of-a-lot to say about how I will play those cards." But I had guidance on how to play my life's cards. A lot of this help was in the form of encouragement from family and Father's base line principles. I'll list the principles stressed repeatedly by Father in a moment. But before I do, please understand that some of Father's principles reflect late nineteen hundred culture; some display a lack of economic knowledge; some were very time limited; some were racist. Other principles are as relevant today as they were when he said them.

I had these working principles as I launched into life. My personal principles would start with many of father's, be augmented by my own and continuously be in a state of change as I traveled

through life. But always, during the course of my life, I would be reflecting upon what Father said about a given situation.

Now for Father's philosophy...

1. Give a man a full day's work for a full day's pay.

2. Talk is cheap. But it takes money to buy whiskey. This translated meant: Keep your promise and promise only what you can and intend to keep.

3. The owner of a company should earn some money for each hired employee in his shop. Otherwise, why would he hire more employees?

4. Don't bite the hand that feeds you.

5. When selling a house or other property, the selling price should be everything that you have invested including taxes paid. (Note: Father had no concept of taxes as a payment towards the cost of shared community services. Neither did he understand inflation nor market value of property.)

6. Show respect to your employer and don't speak poorly of him. After all, he did hire you thus providing the income to support yourself and those dependents upon you.

7. The country should have stayed on the gold standard. Currently paper money has nothing behind it so it has no real value. Also, the only good Sunday newspaper is the Chicago Tribune. Father didn't like those liberal Milwaukee newspapers.

8. Don't buy a used car. You're only buying someone else's problems.

9. You should keep your automobile until the amount you receive in trade equals the purchase price less one-dollar depreciation for each day you owned the car.

10. Birds of the same feather flock together. You don't see a robin mating with a bluebird do you? God never meant for Black people and White people to marry. Likewise, chose your friends from among those who: have similar moral standards and ethical values; are, like you, ambitious by having a desire to achieve and get ahead in life; have similar or higher level of education; and similar or higher social status. (This translated meant: You are judged by the company you keep.)

11. Don't get married until you have completed your education, have a permanent job, own a house and money in the bank.

I moved a dime from my change pile over to him. He ordered a wine. I quickly picked up my change, drained my glass and left. Now I knew. This wasn't a plush cocktail lounge. The bartender knew change on the counter meant a "hit" by a local drunk.

Father's philosophy, a lot of which I adopted, allowed one error. From now on I would be more observant of my surroundings. When in a strange place I would watch who and what was around me. It's not that I minded giving a dime to a drunk for a wine. But allowing people in a skuzzy place to know I had money and came in alone was asking for trouble. Another lesson learned on this tour.

Another active duty tour to the eastern coast gave me a chance to spend a weekend in Boston. There were three of us. We slept at the local YMCA, which put up cots at 11:30 PM charging only one dollar per person. Our valuables could be checked in at the desk and were secure.

In Boston we saw: USS Constitution, Old North Church, Paul Reveres house, Kings Chapel, Bunker Hill Monument, Old South Meeting House, Old State House, Copp's Hill burying ground, Granary burying grounds and horse drawn vegetable wagons. The latter at Hay Market Square. I believe my interest in history was activated that weekend.

When stationed at Norfolk Naval Yards a few of us visited Jamestown and Colonial Williamsburg. We were impressed by all that we saw but the one thing that shocked me was seeing 'White Only' and 'Colored Only' signs outside restrooms. I had read about this but seeing is believing.

I should add one more name. During my stay at the Oshkosh Naval Reserve Center my unit officer was Commander Raymond Ramsden. This is a person who I would be involved with well into the 70's. He taught at UWO and I did take a class from him. Later, when I returned as a faculty member, I would actually be on his staff when he became Vice Chancellor.

The Naval Reserve active duty tours provided me the opportunity to see some of our great country. This permitted me to leave my confined and protected surroundings and experience aspects of life unknown to me. And to have these experiences with fellow sailors providing security was terrific.

12. If you make a mistake it isn't your fault. But if you make the same or similar mistake a second time it is your fault. Also worded, "Once burned but not twice burned." Father also used this principle in other ambivalent ways. These were, "Be willing to try new things but learn from your mistakes" and, the cautionary statement, "A bird in hand is worth two in the bush."

13. Get an education. Upward mobility is dependent upon an education. It is important to rise above your roots.

14. If you want something done well, do it yourself.

15. Never quit a job unless you are already hired for another.

My maternal grandfather, Charles Damsheuser, lived with us from 1941 to his death in 1946. During this time, my paternal grandmother, Sophia Hansen, lived alone in the house in which she raised her family. Grandpa Hansen died in 1916. Grandma was 76 when I was born and died in 1954 at the age of 93. Her sons and daughters provided food daily and care when needed since 1916. When she broke her hip at age 89, her daughter Anne moved from California and lived with her for the final four years. My father was very devoted to her and I have many memories helping him transport food to her home. My parents' treatment of my grandparents would remain with me for a lifetime.

at best, be a long shot to receive a scholarship given the requirement of at least three years of teaching experience.

I applied to all seven. To my amazement I received scholarships from San Diego State University, University of Minnesota and University of Kansas. Furthermore I was first alternate at Notre Dame University and Louisiana State University.

The University of Kansas was chosen by process of elimination. San Diego was eliminated because Ginny was now pregnant again and I didn't want the added problems and responsibility involved in transporting a pregnant woman and a one year old child approximately 2500 miles across the country. Furthermore, coming home for Christmas or visits from relatives would be almost impossible. Transportation was laborious in 1959. Air travel was by propeller driven airplanes and the interstate road system wasn't started until the early '60's.

My problem with the University of Minnesota was Minneapolis. I wasn't ready for big city living.

The University of Kansas had about thirteen thousand students and located in a city of twenty-six thousand. Yet it was a big name school, played athletics in the Big Eight conference and was about 650 miles from Appleton. The mathematics department chairman at UWO had attended KU so I knew a lot about the school. He would talk about KU in the classroom.

I talked to the superintendent of schools of the Wausau Public Schools requesting a leave of absence. This was not their policy so I simply resigned. This was an opportunity that I couldn't pass up. I knew I would be very marketable after completing the program at KU.

We sublet our Wausau apartment furnished to a teacher at the Catholic high school in town, packed a U-Haul trailer and left for Kansas.

University of Kansas

Our housing at KU was prearranged for us. We would stay in married student housing at a complex called Stouffer Place. Each red brick building had eight units all with outside entrances. Four were on ground level and four on second floor. The lower four were reserved for couples with children. The buildings were all

within walking distance of the campus.

The units were small. Ours had two bedrooms, a bathroom, small living room and a galley kitchen. Yet it was our most modern apartment to date.

Many of our institute members also lived in Stouffer Place. This made making new friends easier. We had so much in common as high school math teachers. The building next to ours housed Don and Ruth Johnson and Frank and Alice Rogers. The Johnson's were from Omaha, Nebraska and the Roger's from East Lansing, Michigan. Currently, over forty-years later, we still exchange cards at Christmas time.

A lot of my time was spent with Don and Frank. We formed a study group to study together between classes at the student union. With Bob DeVinney, our study team enlarged to four.

The Johnson's had a twelve-year-old daughter who became Lee's babysitter. This certainly was convenient. We didn't have to find and pick up a sitter. Also, the sitter had her mother close by if she needed help.

We enjoyed immensely the diverse activities available on the KU campus. These included Big Eight football and basketball and all the events put on by the theater department.

Lee learned to walk by thirteen months so he was walking by the time we arrived in Kansas. The good news is that our surroundings were very safe for kids. The bad news is that Lee was the exploring type. He had to see everything, touch everything and, yes, taste everything.

Laundry was done in the complex owned coin operated laundry. Returning one day we noticed that Lee had something protruding from between his lips. Pinching his cheeks to force him to open his mouth, we were surprised to be greeted by a large beetle walking out on his tongue. I'm sure glad the head of the beetle was facing us.

The Institute of fifty members had two minorities. These were two Blacks consisting of one male and one female. The four of us mentioned earlier had formed a study team. Our group was a group of convenience since we lived close to each other. While four is a sufficiently large study group, we felt moved to include the Black male, Jimmy Thomas, who, because of race, may have trouble being accepted by another study team.

This was my first close experience with a Black so I found myself very conscious of his involvement in our group.

One day we were walking down Jayhawk Blvd, the main street which bisects the campus, I spotted a young coed who was....ah....shall I simply say, "well stacked". I mused and said to my companions, "Too much sail for such a small craft." Frank, Don and Bob looked and laughed at my comment. Jimmy looked and then looked away with an expressionless face. I concluded, rightly or wrongly since we made no attempt to talk out what Jimmy was feeling, that Jimmy didn't feel we would accept him if he joined poking fun of a White woman or even enjoy our harmless bantering of the situation. I felt very sorry for Jimmy since we accepted him but yet must have felt it was a token offer made to a Black man and not a relationship inclusion. I began to understand what years of discrimination must have done to the Black community.

We did attempt one social function with Jimmy, which also ended awkwardly.

The Detroit Tigers were playing the Kansas City Athletics in KC one pleasant spring evening. We drove over only to experience a real downpour enroute. Arriving at the ballpark we found it empty and concluded, correctly it turned out, the game was called because of rain.

Not wanting to return to Lawrence without some evening activity, we looked for a restaurant. Finding one we parked the car and proceeded into the small café, the type often referred to as a 'greasy spoon' restaurant. It was long and narrow with stools fixed to the floor before a long counter, which ran the full length of the room. Booths lined the wall on the other side. Behind the counter was a wall covered with mirrors.

The others, who were from communities with sizable Black populations, should have known the meaning of the large sign attached to the mirrors, which read:

WE RESERVE THE RIGHT TO REFUSE SERVICE

The five of us seated ourselves at the counter and began ordering. When the waitress got to Jimmy she said: "Now this is 'to go' isn't it?" Jimmy responded, "No".

They delivered the food promptly to the four of us who were

White. We started eating not wanting the food to get cold. Then they brought Jimmy's food in a brown paper bag stapled shut by at least twenty staples. I was dumbfounded, "How could they do this?", I thought. This was 1959. Long after the Emancipation Proclamation and separate but equal laws were unconstitutional. I had little concept of southern segregation.

Don and Frank didn't hesitate and quickly gave marching orders.

"We're leaving. Leave your food. Pick up your bill and pay the appropriate amount."

We left. No one said a word about the incident in the car as we drove back to Lawrence.

All too soon our year in Kansas was drawing to a close. Many of us stayed for a summer session after the academic year, myself included, completing a Master's degree.

I tried to return to Wausau but someone who wanted to stay had filled my job. The job I settled on was in Manitowoc, which is only about fifty miles from Appleton and located on Lake Michigan. Manitowoc Public Schools had a good reputation and the city was similar to Wausau and Appleton.

My desire now was to pick a good school system and then work into the job I wanted. "Manty" was willing to cooperate. I would teach two years in a junior high before moving to their senior high.

Scott's Birth

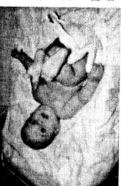

Wasn't Scott a cute baby? The clever use of his foot prevents the showing of too much. He was born October 24, 1959.

"Ed. Eeeeeed, wake up!"

"I didn't hear the alarm."

"It didn't ring yet but I'm having labor pains."

"You can't do that. I have an exam this morning. Just stop it until tonight."

To both of our amazement the pains got

headed for New Orleans.

Our first task after arriving in New Orleans was to find our apartment and to get the key from the owner. We had agreed, through the mail, to sub rent the upper apartment occupied by a female professor at the women's college adjacent to Tulane University.

The apartment owner, Dr. Lyons, lived in the lower apartment. He was eighty-six years old and a retired professor from Tulane. Even at his advanced age, he still taught one astronomy course each semester. This tells you how alert he was.

The house was of a boxy type structure narrow in front and longer going away from the street, locally called 'shot gun' houses—with green shutters and two screened porches one above the other consuming the front of the house. Incidentally, house construction in New Orleans is almost always narrow in front because the footage of the house facing the street is used for taxation purposes instead of its square footage.

We knocked on Dr. Lyons door. I usually let Ginny do the talking when we are in this type of situation.

"Come in."

"We're the Hansens' from…….."

"Say no more. You're sub letting the upstairs while Miss Smith is away for the summer. Welcome to New Orleans. How was your trip?"

"Oh it was fine. But we're tired and the kids need to be fed. Perhaps we could talk more in a day or two. Could we just pick up the key at this time."

"Certainly. One question first. Did Miss Smith tell you about the housekeeper who comes once a week?"

Ginny made these arrangements so she responded, "Yes she did. She said she is a Black lady…….."

"Hold it right there. You're in the South now and as they say 'In Rome do as the Romans do'. This is your first lesson. Never ever call a Black female a lady. That term is reserved for Whites. They're simply Black women."

This was a real lesson for us. We now became very sensitive to southern black issues. From this point on we would tread lightly when race was concerned.

This doesn't mean that we had to abandon our principles on the issue of race. Just that we had to be very discrete when talking to southerners.

The Black woman who cleaned the apartment was paid the standard rate of eight dollars a day plus bus fare. She would bring a bag lunch and eat it sitting outside on the back steps. One week Ginny asked the woman to join her at the kitchen table.

"No missus, I can't do that," was her response. So Ginny joined her outside on the steps so they could eat together. Ginny reasoned, southern traditions might restrict where a Black woman is permitted to eat but it doesn't restrict where a White woman eats.

The second floor apartment consisted of two bedrooms with a bathroom between them on one side, the middle was a long narrow living room with floor to ceiling bookcases and dining room and kitchen on the other side. The kitchen had a swinging door separating it from the dining room.

Scott is looking at Lake Pontchartrain. New Orleans is sandwiched between this lake and the Mississippi River. Scott was one year ten months old and even then we knew that in high school he would anchor the offensive line for the Oshkosh North Spartans. Ginny took the boys swimming almost every day.

One Saturday morning we were awakened by noises coming from Lee and Scott's bedroom. Remember now that Lee had just turned three and Scott was one year nine months old.

Going into their bedroom we found Lee had already been feeding Scott and was now bathing him. Scott was still in his crib and somewhere. Do you see where I made a mistake?"

Invariably he would say something like, "The tenth line down in the development you treated a positive sign as though it were a negative sign. Everything beyond that point is in error."

I really appreciated having him around.

Whenever a class has a 'curve breaker' the class members soon know who it is. My singling out Brian for help wasn't telling them anything they didn't already know.

However, it was a tough pill for the class to swallow. They had to study their butts off and here was a high school kid getting the best grade in class while not even paying attention to the lectures nor doing homework.

While I always enjoyed having a genius in the class, I also realized that his learning was not because of me but in spite of me. My contribution as a teacher would be with those who were learning because of my assistance as a manager of learning.

When I arrived at UWO as a new faculty member in 1963, the key administrative leaders were individuals who moved up the ranks. They were not individuals who were brought in from the outside.

These individuals included Drs. Ray Ramsden, James Duncan and Sherman Gunderson. I had all three of them as professors in the 1950's, knew them personally and liked all three.

The only major infusion from the outside was Chancellor Robert Guiles who replaced Dr. Forest Polk in 1962.

To say that the bureaucracy was inbred would be an accurate statement. This led to some amusing things. Like the letter written by Dr. Duncan in 1962 indicating how out of touch he was in current dress trends throughout the nation. I provide the complete text.

March 1, 1962

To the Men of the Faculty:
Subject: Proper appearance

The reactions herein expressed grew out of the recent visitation by a representative of the American Association of University Women looking towards recognition of our college by that organi-

zation. As we conducted our visitor about and presented her to various faculty members, we became more and more concerned with the impression created by our appearance.

I suppose that every man at times has fancied himself on a lonely island or in a remote wilderness where it would not be necessary to shave his face, to button his shirt, or to strangle his throat with a tie. A college campus is not sufficiently remote to permit the indulgence of such fancies.

We instruct our student teachers to appear in their classes in suits and ties and polished shoes. Can we afford to do less? It seems to me that the classroom is the sanctuary of learning and that we should be as careful of our appearance there as we are in the sanctuary of a cathedral.

Long established custom has set the matched suit, white shirt and tie as the preferred dress. Less desirable but still acceptable is a garb consisting of slacks, jacket, tinted shirt and tie. Hot summer days might dictate the removal of coat or jacket and appearance in shirtsleeves but this should be regarded as a concession to unfavorable environment and not the mode of good taste. Laboratory and shop may dictate protecting smock and activities classes in physical education call for dress designed for the activity.

Large universities may tolerate a few eccentrics who delight in a bizarre appearance of unusual haircuts and beard growths, open shirts, and colored vests, but in colleges the size of ours, there should be no encouragement of the beatnik whose marks are unkempt hair and beard and slovenly dress.

It seems, too, that good taste should prevail on the street as well as in the classroom, on the tennis court as well as on the campus. Bermuda shorts and bathing trunks may be appropriate on the golf course or bathing beach but seem decidedly out of place on the street or on the campus.

My appeal is: let us give some thought to the impression we create by our appearance, keeping in mind that in a teacher training institution our students take courses in us as well as in academic disciplines.

James F. Duncan
Dean of the College

CHAPTER 8 C
November 21, 1963

For many reading these memoirs the happenings of the 1960 to 1970 decade are not even a distant memory. In this episode and the next I will briefly sketch the broad picture of this decade so what I will say fits into context.

We moved from Manitowoc to Oshkosh in August 1963. While we were familiar with the city, how long we would stay was unknown. For this reason we chose to rent an apartment.

Two brand new four-plex row house apartments would be entirely occupied by newly recruited UWO professors. Our building, besides us, housed Doug Kilday, Wayne Wallace, Bruce Black and their families. The apartments in pairs were reflective congruent to the adjacent one. Our unit had this relationship to one occupied by Bruce and Becky Black. We became good friends and Bruce and I would commute together to UWO.

This is how it happened. Bruce and I were commuting together in Bruce's car November 21, 1963. I was talking and oblivious to the fact that our musical program on the car radio had been interrupted. Bruce cut into my conversation saying, "Please be quiet. I want to listen to the news flash."

The newscaster was giving sketchy details of the assassination of President John F. Kennedy. The assassin, Lee Harvey Oswald, would later be gunned down by Jack Ruby. Oswald was even in custody when killed. The 60's violence was just ratcheted up.

Broad Picture

On the national scene the ill-fated Bay of Pigs invasion of Cuba by Cuban exiles backed by the US CIA occurred in 1961. But there is more. By fall 1962 the Soviet Union had moved missiles to Cuba. Disclosed by surveillance planes, the US blockaded Cuba and prepared to invade it. This war was averted when the Soviet Union agreed to dismantle the missile bases in exchange for a US concession to not invade Cuba.

Also in 1962 the Soviet Union built a 28-mile wall separating East and West Berlin. Other borders were also closed. Now an 'iron curtain' separated Europe.

On the domestic front violence began to reign. Black society

demanded what the courts granted in 1954—integration. No longer could the White community practice illegal segregation.

In 1960 lunch counter sit-ins forced desegregation of restaurants. 1961 saw the courts integrate interstate bus terminals. Federal troops integrated the University of Mississippi in 1962.

In 1963 Martin Luther King had his famous "I had a dream…" speech at the Lincoln Memorial. Five years later he was dead from an assassin's bullet while in Memphis.

Peaceful sit-ins and protests became violent as Blacks torched the Watts area of Los Angeles, Detroit and, between 1965 and 1968, spawned more than 100 urban riots.

Back on the national scene, President Lyndon Johnson in 1964 misrepresented facts and convinced congress to pass the Gulf of Tonkin Resolution. This permitted the US to enter, on a massive level, what became 'The Vietnam War'. Soon half a million troops were committed. Body count and Agent Orange became household terms.

By 1968 Vietnam War protesting became ugly when thousands gathered for an angry and violent confrontation with Chicago police at the National Democratic Convention. Burning draft cards, moving to Canada to avoid being drafted and flag burning became common.

1968 also saw College campuses in a state of insurrection. Civil disobedience became the norm as students protested over civil rights, the war, free 'love' and wanting more input into decisions affecting their lives.

The killing hadn't stopped. Malcolm X was gunned down in 1965 and presidential aspirant, Robert Kennedy, in 1968.

US troops spread into Cambodia in 1970. This sparked rioting on 300 college campuses with National Guard troops killing four students at Kent State University.

Never before have Americans killed so many of its leaders, rioted as often, burned so many cities, occupied college buildings or conducted itself in such civil disobedient ways.

November 21, 1968

I want to now focus on how the turbulent 60's spilled onto the Oshkosh campus during the fall semester of 1968. Oshkosh became a microcosm of greater society.

Rumors had circulated since September that the Black population was unhappy, having academic difficulties, complaining repeatedly about their financial aid and were meeting regularly as a Black Student Union. To the ordinary professor not in the official pipeline it was just that, rumors. It's not that we totally dismissed the rumors, they just weren't directed at us so we went about our business of teaching.

Thursday November 21, 1968 started out just like any other day. The commute from home to my third floor Dempsey office was chilly but normal for November. My office was a temporary cage type built along the third floor corridor. Metal walls were seven feet high with screening continuing to the ceiling. They were secure from intruders, provided eye blockage from the corridor but were not sound proof. Tom Eierman had the office next to me and we had removed our separating partition to see each other while we conversed.

About nine in the morning I heard a large commotion on second floor followed by the sound of the fire alarm. This was followed by Tom running into his office. Panting he exclaimed; "We must evacuate our offices and the entire Dempsey building. This is no drill! The Black students are rioting in President Guiles' office. I don't mean one or two students but the whole group."

Tom grabbed a couple of textbooks, some papers to grade and his grade book. Slamming his office door he was off running. Noticing that I hadn't started moving by the time he left he exclaimed as he ran, "Now, Ed... NOW, ED".

Soon the muffled sound from his running feet ended. I reached over to the light switch and flipped off the lights and pushed the button locking the door. I was now all alone in my dark locked office.

While I discovered my underarms becoming moist I had no intentions of leaving. Things were happening and I didn't want to miss them. I quickly called Ginny to appraise her and tell her to watch TV. Then I sat in the cold gray darkness.

After about fifteen minutes I heard footsteps. They seemed to stop and start repeatedly. With the sound alternating between decreasing and increasing I concluded the person was changing di-

rections by going into open rooms. The sound continued getting closer and closer. It dawned on me that someone was checking rooms looking for people. It probably was the police.

I heard no doors opening and closing. Finally the sounds were passing my office door and, as I held my breath, continued down the corridor. I was still secretly hidden in my office. Once the sounds disappeared I never heard any more footsteps nor sounds of any kind.

An hour or so later I slowly opened the door and seeing no one, stepped out. Slowly and very quietly I walked down the corridor. The stairwell going down to the second floor had a landing half way down permitting the steps to turn 180 degrees. They then continued to the second floor. Windows at the landing provided viewing of the campus. I proceeded to the windows and gazed out.

Helmeted Club-Carrying Police

I shuttered thinking, "Good God it's a war zone!" Helmeted club-carrying police were marching from three directions towards Dempsey Hall. Hundreds of students and faculty milled around outside.

President Guile's office was a front office—facing the main street bisecting the campus—in the middle of the second floor. Outside the office door, two corridors met. One was parallel to the outside main street while the second emanated from Dr. Guile's office and was perpendicular with the first forming a T.

Soon more than one hundred helmeted club-carrying policemen lined both sides of the second corridor. Silence fell as a policeman with a bullhorn announced, "This is your last opportunity. Come out peacefully or we'll come in to get you." I had the best observation seat as I squatted on the landing between second and third floor.

After a brief silence punctuated by shouts, "You Honkey" and "White devils" the Blacks came out one at a time to be grabbed on each side by policemen and marched outside. Thousands of students had gathered outside watching the Blacks loaded into a Hertz rental truck for transportation downtown. Eighty-nine Black students were arrested. All arrested were from Milwaukee.

I was shocked to learn that the Black Student Union sacked several offices pulling records out of files and throwing the contents around, overturned furniture, damaged typewriters and business machines, pulled pictures off the walls and wrecked them, spilled ink on carpets, ripped books, broke busts on pedestals and broke windows. All this after President Guiles refused to sign a statement of their demands.

The University was effectively closed down first by the riots and then repeated bomb threats. In early evening 2,000 students marched from Reeve Memorial Union to the courthouse. Adding fuel to the fire was busloads of NAACP Commandos from Milwaukee and Black People's Alliance from Madison. All this activity gave license to student and faculty liberals to promote their platforms and to have an audience for further demonstrations. Local students groups included Students for a Democratic Society (SDS).

Thursday's newspaper front-page headlines were: "UWO Offices Torn by Rampant Negroes". It was now not just a campus problem but one that quickly involved the community and state. National publicity followed.

And not the kind the campus wanted. Both NBC and CBS featured the riot on national evening telecasts.

On Friday President Guiles suspended all students arrested for participating in the demonstrations. Following pre-dawn conferences with police the campus was closed and all classes cancelled for a long ten-day Thanksgiving recess. A hard line approach had been taken.

Campus Upheaval

Liberal opposition to the hard line approach was immediate. Liberal faculty taking the radicals position included: Dr. Robert Delk, Dr. David Roth, Bruce Black and Thomas White.

Informational meetings were held by the administration to inform faculty about facts and what was being done. Radicals organized additional meetings (illegal according to the administration) to promote reinstating the Black students and campus change.

The weekend before the first classes, December 7th and 8th, saw a flurry of activity. Tom White and Bruce Black tried to convince the administration to permit their Monday classes to be Black fo-

rum classes. Both were forced by Dr. Ramsden to sign statements that this would not occur.

Liberal students had requested an all school convocation for Monday, December 9th. This was refused. Dr. David Roth held a mock student convocation attended by six hundred students on the Dempsey Hall lawn. He provided an empty chair where, he claimed; Dr. Guiles should be sitting.

Most rank-and-file faculty quickly tired of the radical students and faculty began to close ranks in support of the administration.

The first faculty petition was by a group called Faculty for Education and Orderly Progress at UWO. Forty faculty members signed this one. A second petition, signed by twenty-four mathematics professors read:

"We believe that all students on this campus have equal rights and responsibilities. We deplore the criminal acts perpetrated against the administration, faculty and students at UWO and the people of the State of Wisconsin on November 21, 1968. Further, we believe that the administration of UWO and the Board of Regents have acted prudently and decisively to date in handling this situation.

"We do not approve of the vocal minority in their efforts to shift the blame to the University and absolve the riot participants of responsibility. We believe that the actions of this vocal minority have served only to prolong the crisis and obscure the real issues.

"We are convinced that a strong positive response by the faculty of this statement of beliefs will expedite an equitable solution."

My name was on this petition.

The Board of Regents decided to take the matter out of local hands and deal with it directly. The meeting, to decide the course of activity, was scheduled for Friday December 7th. The Board of Regents meeting in Madison was given a first hand view of the problem when radical students broke past security policemen and invaded the meeting making outlandish demands.

Black Students Expelled

The Board of Regents voted to hire former Supreme Court Justice Ward Rector to serve as fact finder. Hearings began Monday,

December 16. On Saturday, December 21, board Vice President Roy Kopp announced the expulsion of 90 Black students and suspension of 4 others.

The liberal faculty member who was the most outspoken, Dr. David Roth, for "poor job performance," was released following the 68 – 69 academic year. The case was settled out of court in August of 1981 for $10,670 damages and all comments about "poor job performance" were removed from his personnel file.

Well what did I think about all this? I have not injected my personal comments since the Nov. 21 riot day.

Racial Problems?

Was this a racial problem? Well....yes, in part. It was also a cultural problem and a problem endemic with the 60's.

The greater Oshkosh area had few, if any, permanent Black residents. Most of the people, like me, were first or second generation Americans of immigrants from Germany, Poland or Scandinavia. Most northern Europeans are stoic, undemonstrative and obedient to authority. They knew in order to get ahead work and sacrifice was necessary. And education was the doorway to upward mobility. That advancing to higher social strata was possible with education.

Parents convinced their children they could determine and control their own destiny. But nothing would be given to them.

When I attended UWO from 1954 – 1958 there was no financial aid, Guaranteed Student Loans or work-study. There was only support from family and your own work efforts.

At this time if you were from a wealthy family you went to a prestigious private university or small liberal arts college. Both are very expensive. In this way students were with their own financial and social class and thus were fraternizing with those of like status. Since many marriage aged students paired off in college, retaining or improving their initial financial and social class became possible. Class movement without this is possible but parents want their children to start out at least at the level they have already obtained.

Think about this. Having attended both types of institutions I

can attest that there is no educational difference.

When I attended UWO we did have scholarships. But to receive a scholarship academic excellence needed to be demonstrated. Sometimes the founder of a scholarship stipulated financial need or specific program of study but always academic excellence.

By 1968 the term scholarship had begun to be corrupted to include any gift of money or, in slang, "free" money. Government financial aid and while appreciated by all was viewed by a minority of individuals as this "free" money.

Students admitted to UWO in the late 60's and throughout the 70's did not have to meet rigorous admission standards. That came in the 80's with the Chancellor Penson era. Thus many students admitted in 1968 had questionable academic backgrounds and government financial aid was dispensed on a need basis only.

The state funding of UWO was based on the number of students attending. UWO was in a tremendous growth period and grew from 3,200 in 1963 to 12,000 in 1971. UWO was more concerned with quantity then academic quality of the student body in the 60's. Building projects preempted the concern for change in academic standards.

In fact, things got so bad UWO became known as UW "zero". Students spent more time drinking than studying. St. Patrick's Day became St. Rowdy's Day as "bums" throughout the state and neighboring states converged on UWO for a day of vandalism, drunkenness and tipping over cars.

The one hundred Blacks expelled from UWO were predominately from inner city areas of Milwaukee based upon the fact that 75 % received financial aid. Inner city education was not known for academic excellence. Thus, unfortunately, even with weak standards, UWO presented an insurmountable challenge for the Black students given their academic background and socially bankrupt inner city upbringing. It simply wasn't a good fit for them at UWO. It was too much diversity too fast for both the Blacks and UWO. Neither side was ready and prepared for the other.

Many Blacks came, I believe, because of the "free" money and not in pursuit of an education. It was a way out of the inner city without going to Vietnam. Unable to compete academically led to frustration. And the 60's gave vent on how to express frustration.

Not wanting to sound prejudiced, may I add that many White students also were in college to avoid the draft. Many professors had students pleading for higher grades. These students didn't want to live with the consequences of not studying, telling the professor, "Is the punishment of Vietnam warranted by my poor performance in your class. You would be responsible for sending me to Vietnam and maybe death."

While I didn't personally resent the "free" money, I did feel

Black Studies Department

This cartoon was nationally syndicated raising the question not whether but when will the average Black be able to handle collegiate academics. It wasn't the publicity that UWO wanted. But it did thrust UWO into the forefront of schools that, perhaps on too large a scale or poor planning, tried. It would take years for both the Whites and Blacks to overcome the trauma and begin to trust each other at UWO.

badly how the Blacks squandered their opportunity and was shocked at what they did. This was not how you thank society for doing its best to provide an opportunity to pull yourself up by the bootstraps. This was not a token gesture. They simply "blew it". The method of expression was fully inappropriate and then compounded by the fact it was a regional university populated by hard working kids from a European type culture. These kids, most of whom were working their way through collage, were not endeared to the Black students or their civil rights cause. Only the radical students "understood".

The experiment by the administration of importing domestic Blacks for an opportunity at education had not only failed but set race relations in northeast Wisconsin back for years.

Black Student Demands

Before I leave this issue allow me to summarize the Black Union demands presented to Dr. Guiles: an Afro-American Center; hiring of Black instructors; courses in Negro history, literature and language; a Black student fund to help finance the center, secure Black speakers and purchase Black literature; removal of the Director of Financial Aids.

The scene was not any better at the Madison campus. Rioting in February of 1969 resulted in the Governor pressing 1200 National Guard troops into action complete with bayonets. Some student disorders numbered 10,000.

Clearly the nation, state and community were experiencing unprecedented civil upheaval.

I can't help but think of Jackie Robinson, the first Black to be allowed to play professional baseball. At a given point in time he was given an opportunity. We all know how hard it was for the White community to allow integration. As they say in Physics, bodies at rest tend to stay at rest while bodies in motion tend to stay in motion. It's also called inertia. Jackie Robinson took full advantage of his opportunity, he succeeded and that paved the way for other Black athletes. He changed cultural inertia. But on November 21, 1968 there were no 'Jackie Robinsons' among the one hundred demonstrating Black students. Just one hundred students who thought more of 'doing their thing' than furthering the Black cause.

He Said, She Said

Several expelled Blacks tried to communicate their side of the story to the community. The church we attended invited several to a potluck dinner to present issues and negate, or at least present their view of comments made in the media. We invited three to our home for a meal a week later for additional information.

Each group had poignant statements that tended to reflect their position. For the Black students they were: harsh, heavy handed, overkill, misunderstood, eradicate Black student population, not concerned with Black views, insensitive administration, they are also taxpayers, have rights, will not negotiate demands, don't want an education designed for Whites—Blacks do exist, what did peaceful demonstrations get Dr. Martin Luther King? For the administration they were: ungrateful, unprepared academically, spoiled, belligerent, uncultured, inappropriate action, don't understand peaceful expression, crude, we can't yield to demands, change takes time and money, administration represents the state, look what we have done for them, and we recruited them.

I read a newspaper article in 1986 where two of the black Thursday participants said, while not proud of what they did, it was necessary to effect change. I think this is hogwash. They did not sacrifice themselves as Jackie Robinson or Dr. Martin Luther King did for the greater good of the Black community.

The changes desired were well on the way by Black Thursday. Change does take time. Budgets are submitted well in advance of their implementation. So I don't credit these one hundred black students with altruistic motives. Instead, I think they were selfish and were trying to bail out of a situation they were unprepared and unwilling to handle. As products of a violent inner city culture they dealt with the problem, as they would back home. Clearly their modus operandi was: blame someone else for your problems, do nothing to help yourself and get violent. They were not martyrs.

The one hundred Blacks of 1968 needed an attitude change before education was possible. It was George Washington Carver who said:

"Ninety-nine percent of the failures come from people who have the habit of making excuses."

Blacks will succeed when they are convinced they can determine and control their own destiny. Never before have they had the opportunity they had in 1968. But it will take later Blacks to succeed.

Perhaps you're thinking the Black issue was over, suppressed, beaten down and eradicated on December 21, 1968. Allow me to jump ahead to 1973.

Five Years Later

President Guiles had retired and was replaced by Chancellor Robert Birnbaum. The associated problems of this administration are the subject of the next chapter. But one situation is relevant to this chapter.

Chancellor Birnbaum felt the way Black Thursday played out was a grave miscarriage of justice. That the Black Union demands should have been addressed immediately—like, sign the demand letter Dr. Guiles and get on with it. It was inconceivable to him that UWO suspended these students. I was dumbfounded by his position.

It was now five years after Black Thursday and all of the demands of the Black Student Union had been implemented before Chancellor Birnbaum's arrival on campus. But it did take five years.

The aftermath of Black Thursday certainly hampered our recruitment of Black students. They lived predominantly in one geographic area in southern Wisconsin and word of what happened certainly was out. According to Chancellor Birnbaum we were stigmatized by how the situation was handled and our first priority was to undo the bad publicity. So much for the riot!

So how is that for a change in philosophy?

What did I think of all this?

With President Guiles I felt compelled to stand up and be counted in support. Now I felt compelled to sit down and shut my mouth. I certainly wasn't opposed to fully integrating the Black community into UWO. But I also believe you live with your predecessors' decisions and when you change philosophy, carry your constituents with you. A leader too far in front will cause the rank-and-file to view the leader as the enemy. I'm afraid that was my view of him, the enemy.

The change in philosophy would not have been difficult for me to deal with except that Ginny became a personal friend of Doris

CHAPTER 10
Perry's Birth

Perry and Dean got along very well together. They shared a bedroom for a while and Dean would be Best Man at Perry's wedding twenty years later.

"Doctor?"

"Yes."

"Do I have a boy or a girl?"

"You have a boy Mrs. Hansen. A boy with a very good sense of humor".

"Sense of humor?"

"Yes. You see he came out with a great big silly smile on his face. Then I noticed that his little hand was all clenched with a fist. I pried open the fist. Guess what I found?"

"What?"

"A little pink birth control pill."

The doctor was making a joke about the fact that Ginny was on birth control pills when Perry was conceived.

Ginny had been having problems with irregular periods. The doctor in Kansas told her to go off the pill to get her regularity back. This, he said, was a common problem when taking the pill for a long time. We were very very very good while she was off the pill.

The doctor failed to tell us the pills' ineffectiveness for sixty days after starting again. During this sixty-day period we made a spring break trip to Dodge City, Kansas. It had been planned for some time. We billed it as our relaxing final Kansas vacation—without kids—before heading back to Wisconsin in June.

I remember traveling in and around Dodge City looking for a motel. Ginny wanted the fancy expensive motel in the center of the city with glitzy lights and a swimming pool. Since I was driving I exercised veto power and we went to a Mom and Pop motel on the outskirts. The outskirts had little entertainment and Mom

Birnbaum, Chancellor Birnbaum's wife. And the Birnbaums lived right on campus in a state provided residence.

Details are found in another chapter but Ginny and Doris both enrolled in the same cooking school in Fond du Lac taught by Madame Kuony. Soon they were commuting together. Thereafter Chancellor Birnbaum, referred to by Ginny as "Bob", was calling our house to have Ginny purchase Christmas and birthday presents for Doris. Madame Kuony sold the equipment necessary for making some of the dishes being cooked. And these would be the presents Ginny was asked to buy. Now all I heard around the house was Doris and Bob this, Doris and Bob that, and so on. I became careful not to answer the phone in fear that 'Bob' would be calling.

For reasons explained in the next chapter Chancellor Birnbaum was very intimidating to me. When Ginny's cooking class was over she enrolled at UWO as a full time student. Between classes Ginny and Doris would have tea and crumpets. Of course they talked about their husbands. I quickly told Ginny I wanted no couple activity, no double dates and no inviting husbands into each other's homes. I felt I must keep my distance. He simply had absorbed too much power. I felt like an ant ready to be stomped on. His complete 180-degree turn from the position Dr. Guiles and Dr. Ramsden had taken on the Black issue was too much for me to handle. After all, I did work for Dr. Ramsden from 1967 to 1972 and the removal of him by Chancellor Birnbaum for 'philosophical reasons' didn't sit well with me.

Then it happened! Ginny told Doris that I had a scrapbook of all of the newspaper articles of Black Thursday, all administrative memos, all student newspaper issues and all petitions signed by faculty members. (That is why this chapter is as complete as it is. I had everything.) And of course 'Bob' wanted to see this scrapbook.

Fortunately the scrapbook was held together with twine. I carefully removed all the petitions which would 'incriminate' faculty including the one with my name. That one would have associated me with Dr. Guile's position. Then I allowed Ginny to lend the book to 'Bob'.

The games we have to play.

157

Well that night in Dodge City, Perry outran 250,000 other players and arrived first at that white ball coming down the fallopian tubes.

When Dean was born Ginny had endured a lot of thoughtless verbal abuse from repeated phone calls from anxious friends and relatives. We had decided we were not going to go through that again. The due date that we publicized was one month after the actual date the doctor thought was correct. Yes, I said thought.

Perry loved to fish. Here, at the age of 6 or 7, he shows off his catch.

On the morning of January 7, 1967, a Saturday, Ginny started labor. We were puzzled because it was one month early. Fearing a problem we called the doctor who had office hours that day. Driving to the doctor's office located in Doctors Park was difficult. An ice storm the previous day left side streets an icy dangerous mess.

The doctor took one look at where Perry was trying to enter the world and said,

"Go directly to the hospital. Do not stop home for the packed suitcase. I'll meet you there."

Our phone calls announcing the birth took everyone by surprise. After all, it was two months before the date we told them. Explaining that Perry was a full term baby and accounting for one lie and a doctor's error eased everyone's concerns.

Many people said,

"Next time we won't believe the date you give us. This would bring a response from us of,

"There won't be a next time. Four is enough."

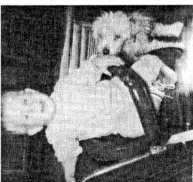

Perry and Miss Hercules were inseparable. They bonded when Ginny fed Perry. Hercules would wrap herself around Ginny's neck. When Perry looked up to see who was providing his nourishment he would see two faces, Mother and Hercules. Hercules and Perry slept in the same bed and the only time they fought was over who got the pillow. Here Miss Hercules is cleaning off Perry's 'gobbie' hand.

and Pop motels in the 1960's didn't even have television. So we made our own entertainment.

Perry's athletic ability started that night. While in high school Perry played soccer. You know that sport where lots of people run around trying to either hip bump, head hit or kick some poor little white ball. (You must remember that soccer in the 1980's was new to the USA.)

Perry is around four years old here. By this time Aunt Kit had passed away. Uncle Otto lived only three houses down the block from my parents. He was a 'regular' at my parents' house taking many meals there. He was a very lovable man and we all loved him dearly. One can just see his radiance as he plays with Perry.

Cubscouts

It was the annual January Cub Scout pack meeting. As a cub pack we always ran the pinewood derby at this event. The father-son project over the Christmas holidays was to build the fastest car under 5 ounces. But this event would be different.

"Boys", I said after the event was run but before we went home for the day,

"I received a call from Gotham City. Now who knows what famous person is from Gotham City?"

It was no surprise when I heard a chorus of boys respond, "Batman."

"That's right, Batman. Now Batman called to request permission to enter his car in the after-glow races. I said `Okay`. Is that alright?"

Lee turned 8 in 1966. By 1967 I had been recruited as Cub Master. When you have four sons with only nine years between the first and the last, you're in for the long haul. Since Scott and Dean were four years apart I had a one-year breather. Actually I really enjoyed my time in Cubbing. I remembered my old Cub Master, Mr. Wilbur Close, and what he meant to me. I wanted to do the same for my sons. I wanted to lead by doing and not by saying. Leadership, sportsmanship, human worth, family fun, respect for the individual and his differences, cooperation are just some of the attributes of the scouting program.

"Yesssssssss."

It took a few more minutes to resettle the boys since they obviously were enthralled.

"Batman's car is at the starting box. But before it runs tell the most unique feature of Batman's car?"

The cubs were really into this run so I had no problems eliciting the response, "rocket powered".

The pinewood derby batmobile was made from the standard kit. A plastic Batman was at the steering wheel and he was very visible through a plastic canopy. Headlights adorned the carved front fenders and yellow on black bat-head images were painted on the wheels. A large dorsal fin was attached on top at the rear by the rockets.

Yes, I said rockets. Most of you know what I mean by a bottle rocket. In its normal use the stick portion is placed in a free standing bottle thus the business end is pointed skyward, the fuse lit and zoom up 'they go' exploding in the air.

There is a second kind of bottle rocket called non-report bottle rockets. These zoom upward leaving a trail of smoke and sparks behind. They do not contain a firecracker and thus are called non-report bottle rockets.

In the back of the batmobile four one-fourth inch holes two inches deep were drilled. Four non-report bottle rockets with sticks broken off were placed in the holes. The fuses were then tied together so that one match would light all four.

After I completed my story about Gotham City and my conversation with Batman, I gave the order to run the Batmobile. Ivan Isaacson was manning the starting gate. He lit the fuses and pressed the start button. Within seconds the rockets ignited propelling the Batmobile down the track at an unbelievable speed spewing smoke

Mothers were asked to pin the badges on their son. This was a family program and mothers were an integral part helping them to pass through the requirements. Here Ginny pins a badge on Perry.

I bought a Santa Claus suit and became Santa Claus at the Cub Scout annual Christmas party. I also visited some of our friend's children. Whenever I was traveling in the car to play Santa I would take extra time and just drive around. When people saw Santa Claus in a car waving to them they invariably broke into a laugh. This helped me get through the feeling that Christmas had become too commercial. In the picture, Santa is sharing 'pearls-of-wisdom' to Perry explaining about delivering presents to everyone the same night.

and sparks along the way. It flew across the gym and stopped by some rugs strategically placed for that purpose.

I'm glad no fire marshal was in the building because we must have violated safety codes with fireworks indoors. The cubs loved it. Fathers loved it. Mothers said, "Boy is it smoky in here and does it ever stink."

All four sons participated in cub scouts. It is an outstanding family centered program and I was personally able to maintain quality control by becoming intimately involved.

The boys were involved in cubbing from 1966 until 1978. I held the position of cubmaster and committee chairman for about nine of those years. As such I wrote the committee meeting agenda. These were our planning sessions and attended by all den mothers and pack officers.

Writing the monthly newsletter permitted me the opportunity to communicate with parents and name names of those assigned to pack meeting responsibilities.

Some monthly pack meetings had set programs. December had

169

the Christmas party and January the pinewood derby. Pack meetings were suspended in the summer but we always sponsored at least two softball teams in the city wide softball league. We won a disproportionate number of citywide championships.

Summer was also the time for our all-pack picnic and day camp at Twin Lakes Boy Scout Camp. At day camp the boys were involved in archery, riflemanship, nature hiking, swimming and a

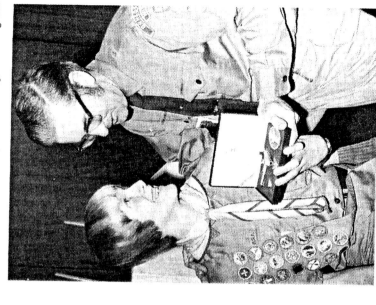

Lee earned the highest award becoming an Eagle Scout. Later in high school he became president of the Police Explorer Post. It was only natural that when he enlisted in the Army he would be in the Military Police. We are all very proud of his accomplishments. Currently, as I write this caption, Lee has been in the Army 20 years and is a Lieutenant Colonel.

170

160

campfire complete with skits.

Soon after becoming involved in cub scouting I purchased my own Santa Claus suit. Not only was I the cub pack Santa Claus but I also visited kids of our friends and occasionally, made visits at Emmeline Cook Elementary School.

One year, when Dean was in third grade, he asked me to visit his classroom Christmas party as Santa Claus. This I did gladly. When finished I went down to the kindergarten. I was greeted enthusiastically and many wanted to be picked up.

Having been the center of attention and enjoying it I went down to the fifth grade. Big mistake. Fifth graders don't believe in Santa Claus.

Shortly after entering the classroom I got sprayed by a stringy plastic substance from a pressurized can. I was flabbergasted; worried that my white beard would be completely messed up. The teacher intervened grabbing the offending student and, much to my amazement, six of my cub scouts—who knew who Santa was—quickly jumped up and picked off the substance. I then promptly exited.

Spaghetti Anyone?

"Mom, when is supper done?" It was Dean and he was hungry.

"Let me see........" With those comments Ginny went to the boiling pot and with a fork extracted one long piece of spaghetti. With a flick of the wrist she flung the spaghetti against the wall where it stayed. She then announced,

"It's done. Call your brothers."

Dean ran from the room yelling to his brothers,

"Mom just threw a piece of spaghetti at the wall and it stuck there!"

The boys came running to see their mother's work of art still clinging to the wall.

"Did you do that?" they chimed.

"Well yes. This is just another way to test spaghetti to see if it's done. Spaghetti not done is hard and will drop to the floor. When it stays, voila, it's done."

Once she started this method of testing she had to keep it up. Sometimes they would try to goad her into throwing early just to

Refugees Sponsored in 1979

November 1979 ushered in a new stage in our lives. That is when the first of six family units walked off the plane in Oshkosh. I intend to do a lot of writing describing our experiences when this book is completed. For now I'll "whet your whistle" with an article written and published by the Tampa Tribune.

WE REMEMBER IT WELL

It was 5 PM when the phone rang. The now familiar female voice said,

"Please help me. My cousins from Thailand come in two hour. My car too small to carry them from airport."

Of course we went and soon the plane landed. We waited hoping all would have coats. November of 1979 was unseasonably cold in Oshkosh, Wisconsin. Soon off walked a mother, father and five daughters ages 3, 5, 7, 9, and 11.

We loaded everyone into the two cars and went to her small spartanly furnished apartment.

"And where will they sleep?" I asked.

The Khamsy Luangpraseuth family arrived from Laos the Monday after Thanksgiving 1979. What a fun time we had together. We blended so well with each other. The picture was taken the summer of 1980 right after Lee returned from the Army.

She pointed to the floor.

"People can't sleep on the floor," I stated with assurance.

"They sleep on floor in refugee camp. It warm and dry on floor."

I had read newspaper articles and heard news reports about "boat people" from Indochina but now it was becoming real. Now "boat people" were coming to Oshkosh.

It was the Monday after Thanksgiving and we had feasted sumptuously at the holiday meal. Seeing these people was a reminder of the Biblical story of the rich man and poor Lazarus. I realized now was our time to share.

Leaving, we quickly returned with our camping supplies of sleeping bags and air mattresses.

"And where is the sponsor?" I asked

"No sponsor. I find no one to sponsor."

This prompted my wife and me to have some very serious conversations. At that time she was on the Church Council. It had been her suggestion the council approve a request to sponsor a refugee family and appoint me as chairman of the project. I quickly organized a committee to research and identify the needs.

Once organized Lutheran Social Services put us in contact with this Laotian woman. She had requested reunification with relatives in refugee camps. She needed the assistance of a sponsor to help assimilate them into the community.

Soon her relatives came. Not one family came but two, a woman and her 18-month-old daughter and a single man. The church agreed to sponsor both small families.

What the woman never told us was that her request was for three families. It was this third family that just arrived. She had hoped to obtain help from another church for them but help didn't materialize.

Our church was overwhelmed with their first two families, requiring two apartments and two sets of furnishings, therefore said 'no' to the third. Could my wife and I, already deeply involved working with the church caring for the first arrivals, take on more responsibility and sponsor this large family ourselves?

After deliberating three days we personally became the sponsors of this seven-member family. We were given vouchers from Catholic Charities valuing $1750 to be used for rent and food. Not

much for so many mouths but it was a start.

We had both husband and wife working within one week despite their not knowing English. In two weeks the family was moved to an apartment. Our money for food was short having to pay rent in advance plus another month's rent for a security deposit.

Both Oshkosh High Schools were contacted. Normally at Christmas, students collected clothes for the needy in the community. This time they identified the refugees as the needy. What we couldn't use we took to the Saint Vincent de Paul Society who, in exchange for the abundance contributed, provided household items still needed by the family.

A local doctor provided free health screening so the children could attend school. Within four weeks the parents were attending evening ESL (English as a second language) classes while my son and I babysat.

By Christmas we had been showing up regularly in church with our greatly enlarged family. Hearts warmed and any concern about the churches over-involvement with refugees dissipated, in fact, the people of the church provided a mountain of toys and I donned my Santa Claus suit to make an appearance delivering the presents on Christmas Eve.

Within six weeks of arrival the children were mainstreamed in the public schools. The evening before classes were to begin my wife instructed the girls on how to say, "Where is the bathroom?" She also attended classes with them until they were adjusted to school.

The family had difficulty understanding why we would help people from across the world. People we didn't even know. Finally the father said,

"We must be cousins. If not, you would not help." Six months later the father, who had been an orphan, said to us,

"You are my father and you are my mother."

We learned that relationship, not only biology, would make a family.

By 1983 we had sponsored the rest of the extended family, another ten Laotians. We obtained jobs for all of them. None were placed on welfare. To all we became know as 'Mom' or 'Dad', 'Grandma' or 'Grandpa' and, now, 'Great Grandma' or Great

Grandpa'. We have been given the title of the roles we play in our extended family.

In 1993 I became ill and my health deteriorated. Soon I was physically handicapped and forced into a premature retirement. Needing time to rest and recuperate we moved to the sunshine filled warm days of Florida. Who moved us? Yes, those we started helping in 1979. They loaded and drove the truck, and settled our belongings in our new condo.

It is almost twenty years after that fateful Thanksgiving phone call. So how about those five little girls? They are beautiful women ages 22, 24, 26, 28 and 30. Four are married with five children among them.

The fifth woman, the one who was 5 in 1979, graduated from college last January and will marry her college sweetheart September 5th of this year. We will travel back to Wisconsin to participate in the wedding and to 'puff' our chests as proud grandparents. And yes, the wedding will be in the same church whose hearts needed warming in 1979.

Most of our Asian relatives have been to Florida at least once for a visit. I introduce my extended family member as, "This is my granddaughter" or "This is my son". The person receiving the introduction isn't expressionless. The eyebrows raise, the mouth opens, and bewilderment crosses the face. But rarely do words get uttered as they look into the brown eyes and black hair on the person standing next to blue eyed blondes. I'm so proud to call them family.

Our bond is strong and our love for each other is great. This clearly was and continues to be some of the most significant times of our lives. Growing older I not only have these pleasant memories but phone calls on Father's Day, birthdays and holidays. And the love of these relatives as they visit us in Florida.

Our Changing Vacation Pattern with Family Needs

Ginny's parents moved to Colorado in 1966 and would live there for the next ten years. But they did a great job of relating to our four sons though living eleven hundred miles away.

They vacationed in Wisconsin each year and always did things with the boys. Each of the boys were able, at least once, to return

235

Starting in 1978 and for the next seven years we spent the spring break week visiting Ginny's parents in Dunedin, Florida. We always converged on them with a mob. Here in 1982 from L - R is Pedro (the younger brother of the Mexican exchange student who lived with us the 1980-81 school year), Perry, Dean, Robin, Scott, June, me and Bert. Ginny took the picture. The picture was taken in 1982.

234

Such beauties they became. They are now 14, 16, 18, 20, 22 years of age. Front row L - R are Thongsone, Thongsouk and Phetsamone. Back row L - R Manikhone and Thipphaphone. Come on Phetsamone, say cheese! The picture was taken in 1990.

163

CHAPTER 17 C
New Office

The Mathematics department moved from Polk Library to Swart Campus School, renamed Swart Hall, when the campus school was disbanded. This happened in the very early '80's. It was a good news-bad news situation. Good news, the Mathematics department had its own building sharing only a few basement rooms with the day-care center. Bad news, it wouldn't be renovated for several years.

Choosing offices was done by seniority within rank. Another perk for the PhD's who could advance into the higher ranks. Thus I had low priority. My office was in a former classroom and shared with two other faculty members.

Changed Offices Again

Some time around 1985 the department decided to repossess my office to use it for seminar classes. The office next door was occupied by John Oman and Jimmy Laken. Jimmy at the time of the repossession, was having back problems which forced him into early retirement.

John was my assistant when I was in charge of the Sunday School at Calvary Lutheran Church. Since John was an old friend and his office had a vacancy. I quickly vacated my office and moved in with John. This office was large and also a former classroom, though not as large as the one I just left. But there was plenty of room for two people.

After getting settled in the new office I noticed a Chinese man, who I will call Chang, roaming daily about the office. He had some tea, soups, cups and a hot plate on a table between my area and John's.

He would say nothing to either one of us; had his own key to the office; read books, magazines or newspapers while in the office; came and went at will and always disappeared if students came into the office to talk to us.

The Resident Chinaman

Finally after about a week, I asked John about him.
"Tell me about Chang. Is he your graduate student?"

"No. In fact he isn't a current student. A former student, yes. He was a foreign student from China and never returned to his homeland. He has his master's degree and never moved on with life. I know little more except he was befriended by Jimmy and now goes with the office. I didn't have the heart to kick him out when Jimmy left."

I was dumbfounded. So we have a resident Chinaman cohabitating with us. No wonder he was trying to be invisible and not upset us.

This presented an interesting situation. Wanting more information I waited for an opportunity and when presented, engaged him in conversation.

Initiating conversation I said,
"Tell me Chang, do you live around here? Ever go back to China? Or, are your family members here? I'm very curious."

"Well, you see, I don't want to return to China. At least not right now. I want to bring my parents to this country. This is possible only if I'm a U.S. citizen."

"What is your immigration status now?"

"Since I'm not a student, my student visa has not been renewed. I am, what you call it? Ah.....an illegal alien."

"Is anyone looking for you?"

"No. I don't think so. U.S. Immigration has better things to do than look for a poor miserable, former Chinese student. As long as I don't call attention to myself I'm okay."

"What is your plan?"

"There has been a law before the U.S. Congress several times. Thus far it has not passed, but if passed when resubmitted, it permits undocumented aliens to become citizens. The requirements appear to include having lived here five years, to work and be self supporting. I am waiting for this law to be passed. Then I'll apply for citizenship and this will open the door to get my parents here."

"Where do you work?"

"I just do odd jobs, any kind of a job where a social security card isn't necessary. I always get a receipt for services rendered so I can prove I work. I also have rented a small bedroom in a house close to campus. Thus I can prove I am self supporting by paying rent. The room is small which is why I'm always here or in the

University library. My free time is all spent reading."

"Are you in contact with your parents?"

"Yes. I have a Post Office box under an alias name."

"Do you have friends or relatives to relate to?"

"No, neither. My relatives are all in China. The friends I had have all graduated and moved away. I haven't kept contact with any of them nor attempted to develop new friends for this reason. No one must know of me, where I am or what I am doing. It takes only one person to complain to Immigration and I will be deported. You see, I must use my real name on the wage stubs and rent receipts if I'm to prove what I must when the law is passed. Only four people know I am in the U.S., Jimmy, John, a sociology professor who is also helping me, and now, you."

I had all the information I needed to know and a lot that would be better if I didn't know should Immigration ever talk to me. Certainly I wasn't going to turn him in. I had great respect and empathy for him and what he was trying to do. Especially at the personal sacrifice he was making.

He was never a bother. Talked only if talked to. Always left when a student or faculty member entered. Since I taught half-time I was only in the office for office hours spending the rest of my time in the Registration Center.

I Moved To Dempsey Hall

After about three more years I vacated the office and went to the Registration Center full time. This was in 1987. I had no intention of returning to teaching so I gave away all of my books letting Chang have first dibs.

I would later find out that he stored his book selections in one of the lockers in the hallway, which were formerly used by students when Swart was an elementary school.

A couple of years later the mathematics department had to vacate the entire building for renovations. This is when the campus police called asking what I wanted done with the books with my name in them found in a locker outside the office. I quickly called John who said Chang had moved to Milwaukee. I then told the police to discard the books.

284

Five Years Later

More years passed until the summer of 1993. One day in July I saw Chang outside the Registration Center in the corridor peering in. I was not working with a student so I left to greet him. Arriving in the corridor he promptly asked,

"The books, those in the locker. What happened to them now that Swart has been renovated and the lockers removed?"

"I'm sorry Chang. John said you moved to Milwaukee so when the police called asking why I hadn't removed them I simply said, 'Discard them. They were left behind accidentally'."

"Oh me, oh my. Everything is gone. First the stuff I left with my sociology professor friend and now the books."

"Did your sociology friend know about your move?"

"No. I try to keep as few people as possible knowing where I am. The stuff I left with him I just assumed would remain there but he gave it all to Saint Vincent de Paul just last week. I even went out to the de Paul retail store to look but they kept following me around so I left. They seemed to be bothered because I'm Asian."

"Look, Roger Herold is chairman of the Saint Vincent de Paul Society. Perhaps he can get you in during closed hours to look for your stuff. Would you like that?"

"Yes, of course."

I explained everything to Roger who was happy to allow Chang to look around while the store was closed. Two hours later the three of us were in the store.

Roger and I sat down to talk while Chang looked around. He found nothing but did appreciate the opportunity to look. The stuff that was brought in about two weeks ago was still in the warehouse. A mammoth room with stuff piled all the way to the ceiling. There was no way he would ever find something. Soon he gave up. At least he had the opportunity to look around when his race wouldn't be a problem.

None of the possessions lost had much monetary value. Books, some awards, a plastic mug he got when seeing his only Brewers game, things as such. But it was his and it was all that he had. It was precious to him. We grieved with him.

I took him to the bus terminal so he could return to Milwaukee. I never saw him again.

285

Christmas 1992

An aspect of humanity that sets us apart from the animal world is memory. Memory is the ability to recall prior occurrences and the associated ability to emotionally relive these past events.

It is not desirable to try to forget all bad memories. In fact, some "bad" memories provide a valuable connection to the past. One memory about Dean that I cherish is our last Christmas together. This is one of my writings that was published by The Tampa Tribune as their 1999 Christmas story special. I provide the complete text for you.

WE REMEMBER CHRISTMAS 1992 WELL

I was eating supper in our Oshkosh, Wisconsin condo when the phone rang. It was my wife, Ginny, calling from Florida.

Excitedly she explained how she poured out her soul to the Winter Haven support group. As she did this she observed a man sitting in the corner. Then he took out a small book and began to write.

When the meeting ended this man handed a paper to Ginny and said, "Now go get that apartment for Dean and yourself". Unfolding the paper she saw it was a check for $2000. Ginny could hardly contain herself.

We began immediately planning to make Christmas 1992 the best and most memorable Christmas ever. It would be our last with our son, Dean. The signs were undeniable.

Almost a year earlier, Dean was in the final stages of that disease which is the scourge of the twentieth century; the incurable terminal disease known as AIDS.

Dean's illness advanced from HIV to AIDS in September of 1991. By 1991 standards, this meant the first life threatening hospitalization for an opportunistic infection. People with AIDS have a compromised immune system. As a result they are unable to combat any infectious intruder.

In February 1992, while we were visiting Dean in Phoenix, we experienced for the first time the ravages and horror of the illness as our third born son became deathly sick. Clearly Dean could no longer work or care for himself. We always believed that a son is a son forever.

In the midst of this forty-day hospitalization, with Dean's per-

mission, we became his caregivers. Getting Dean back to Wisconsin was now our next priority.

We arranged to have Dean flown from Phoenix to the University of Wisconsin Hospital and Clinics in Madison, Wisconsin, a distance of over 2000 miles.

The final leg of this trip was a 168-mile ambulance ride from O'Hare airport in Chicago to the Madison hospital. Fog had closed all airports north of Chicago.

While the prognosis was bleak—at most thirty days to live—Dean showed amazing resilience and desire for life. He proved the prognosis wrong.

When released from the hospital the three of us moved into the Oshkosh condo, thankful for more time. We would now have quality time to renew our relationship.

By October, after several more life threatening illnesses with the accompanying hospitalizations, cold fall winds began blowing across Wisconsin.

Dean, acclimated to the warm Phoenix weather and now suffering with a constant fever, made a request. "Could I," he asked, "spend the cold winter months in Lakeland where Grandma and Grandpa live?"

Dean knew his time on earth was very limited. In addition to getting out of Wisconsin for the winter months, he wanted to visit Disney World, Universal Studios and Busch Gardens.

This was a difficult request for us to deal with. It wasn't the location that was the problem, but the money.

Multiple plane rides to Phoenix, an ambulance ride costing $1376 and medications costing $1000 per week were only some of the expenditures.

The expenses not covered by insurance had depleted our savings. Dean's grandparents accepted Dean and Ginny in their home. But their retirement trailer park would only permit visitors to stay for thirty days.

Our belief has always been that love in action is the only kind of love there is. That life isn't lived by a script. And life is lived knowing only the next step.

Ginny and Dean left in mid October for Lakeland, Florida. They were grateful for the hospitality. But three generations living together is not easy and is complicated when one has a terminal disease.

By early December Ginny and Dean had exceeded the permitted time. This is when Ginny ventilated to the support group saying, "What do I do?"

While a single anonymous donor provided the money, the entire support group was involved furnishing the apartment sharing what little they had. We were touched by the generosity of those suffering with this deadly disease. A brotherhood and mutual admiration flourished among us. They were putting shoe leather to the words; "I love my brother."

I already had my plane ticket to fly to Florida when Ginny called. Now I packed a special box of Wisconsin cheese and sausage for our festive time together. On December 22nd I flew to Florida.

Dean's oldest brother and his wife drove from their army base in Virginia to join us in Florida. The stage was now set for our very special Christmas.

Christmas day, also Dean's 29th birthday, was to be spent in the apartment. We planned an open house for all that are infected, disenfranchised, living a secret or in any way affected by AIDS. All were welcome. There was room in this twentieth century inn.

The open house was scheduled for 11AM to 6PM. Already by 10:30AM the first guest arrived, a man in his mid-thirties. His grandmother had raised him. Since he acquired AIDS she didn't allow him in her house. Now he lived with his mother who had to work on Christmas. He was looking for a place to go, a place where people would accept him, and allow him to share in their Christmas celebration.

Another couple spent several hours with us. Their son died a year earlier. Everyone, including relatives, were told it was cancer, but the cancer was caused by AIDS. The wife worked as a dental hygienist. She was concerned that, if the patients found out her son lived with her, they would fear getting AIDS from her cleaning their

Dean wanted a cherry pie instead of a birthday cake. Here he is shown complete with two pies and a 'two' and a 'nine' candle. The date is Christmas day 1992 at the rental condo in Lakeland, FL.

300

Everyone who attended Dean's birthday-Christmas open house, instead of a birthday card, signed the bedspread-size white material. Called his 'Love spread,' it was on his hospital bed when he died May 23, 1993. He is shown here with Lee and Julia who drove down from Ft. Monroe, VA to spend the holidays with him.

301

167

teeth. If this happened, she would have lost her job. They were still living the secret.

These were typical stories told by those attending the open house. We were honored to be the catalyst for their Christmas celebration.

At mid afternoon we celebrated and sang, "Happy Birthday". Dean did not want a cake for his birthday; he wanted a cherry pie instead. This we provided complete with a candle.

In addition to all the visitors, Dean received phone calls from Oshkosh, Green Bay, Phoenix and Pittsburgh. Thirty-five Christmas cards arrived from friends alerted to his situation by the local Oshkosh newspaper.

Ginny wanted a memento of this event and something, when the going was rough, to remind Dean of the people who loved him. She bought a bedspread—sized piece of white material and a set of marking pens. Every person attending the open house, instead of bringing a birthday card, autographed the spread and communicated what Dean meant to them. It became his love—spread.

It was a great day for all of us. Almost everyone who meant anything to Dean had been there or phoned. And Ginny and I have this wonderful memory of Dean's last birthday.

The love—spread, signed with love, enveloped Dean daily and was on his hospital bed when he died five months later.

People affected by AIDS may want to read my book, A Father's Story: The Story of a Son's Battle with AIDS. Contact any bookstore with the ISBN number 0-7880-0663-0 stating Ingram's as the distributor, or my web site, www.aidskilledmyson.com.

Dean Remembered

The last of everything. Shown here are ten pictures of Dean all taken during the last five years of his life. I hope I have included everyone's last remembrances of him.

Morris Hampton

I enjoy reading history and learning how great men did their job. In the battle at Chancellorsville during the Civil War Confederate General Stonewall Jackson was wounded resulting in the amputation of his left arm. Before complications of pneumonia claimed his life, General Robert E. Lee said, "He has lost his left arm, but I have lost my right."

Lee and Jackson fit like a hand in a glove. Lee said of Jackson, "Such an executive officer the sun never shone on. I have but to show him my design, and I know that if it can be done it will be done. No need for me to send or to watch for him. Straight as the needle to the pole he advances to the execution of my purpose." To follow in Lee's executive footsteps the lesson is clear: Find your Stonewall.

When I took over the job of coordinator of advisement for the College of Business Administration I was blessed with my Stonewall, Morris Hampton. I now had what I didn't have as COLS Coordinator. To be able to leave the office and fully realize Morris would be able to service whatever need might arise. I can't say enough about how Morris made my job so much easier.

While Roger did require Morris to handle some duties unrelated to Business, I always had Morris when I needed him and I had his thinking time. He was always coming up with ways to improve our procedures. How to display requirements on our planning sheets was a specialty of his. Morris was always thinking business.

When I was the COLS Coordinator the COLS advisors were either faculty half time or coaches. Most of the faculty, and all of the coaches, would spend thinking time on their academic teaching subjects or recruitment issues and other sport activities. With Morris I had him 100% of the time.

Personally, Morris and I always got along marvelously. Professionally we seemed to compliment each other. If our advisees wanted youth, they had Morris; age (like good wine) they had Ed and so on.

Seriously, I must reiterate that Morris was a tremendous asset. He also had expertise in areas where I had none. Specifically, I knew "dittlely" about computers.

THE OFFICE REPORT

Current issue : How computers provide information at your finger tips.

The Newspaper of the Advisement /Registration Center

Ed Hansen using his new computer

Many times Computer Service personnel would be in my office to discuss our role in certain procedures under development. People who spend their day before a computer develop a language called computereze, or to my ear, computer babble. Morris, who had training on computers, became my translator. Conversations would go like this:

Morris: "Ed, CS is here to explain changes in the Student Progress Summaries."

Ed: "Great! I'm anxious to hear about them."

CS: "First you....blah, blah, blah...RAM...time study....megahertz....blah, blah.....study ergonometics at the whatchamacallit."

Morris: "Ed, CS says that we can list a course twice, once each in the appropriate major areas."

Ed: "Great! Now how about listing both our names for the student advisor so the students have a choice?"

CS: "Yadda, yadda,.....some networking.....yadda, yadda, yadda....point-and-click the mouse at the thingamajig."

Morris: "Ed, CS says it can be done."

Ed: "Good. We're making progress. Can we put the student registration date on the Summary?"

CS: "Blah, blah, blah....damn virus....blah, blah, blah...purchase new software...special font.....aim the new joystick at the doohickey."

Morris: "Ed, the answer is yes."

Ed: "Fine. What else do we have?"

CS: "Bada-bing the ....yadda, yadda, yadda....bimbos in the office....megabytes....Can you play solitaire yet?"

Morris: "Ed, CS is wondering what your level of expertise and computer literacy is?"

Turning staring at the wall keeping my mouth closed but having understood the word 'solitaire' I thought: 'Tell'em to step in a bucket of cement and jump off the Brooklyn bridge.

Ed: "I'm working on it."

Morris, good buddy, if you ever read this book please accept a big 'THANK YOU.' You really made my seven years in the office as COBA Coordinator a pleasure . Thank you, thank you.

The Freshman Registration Problem

Have you ever gone to a pot-luck supper and been the last table chosen to get food? Sure, we all have. So we all have had the experience of seeing the food before tables were called and what remained when we had our turn.

We console ourselves by saying, "It was the luck of the draw. After all, we could have been first."

But how do you feel if you're a senior in high school registering for college freshmen classes and the buffet of courses is either gone or totally cannibalized when your turn comes? This was a regular occurrence at UWO.

Incoming freshmen need courses for General Education and, in some cases, to meet requirements in their major. The three professional colleges have such extensive course requirements that few elective courses are needed. Counting these elective courses on

329

330

THE UW-O TATTLER

THE UW-O TATTLER

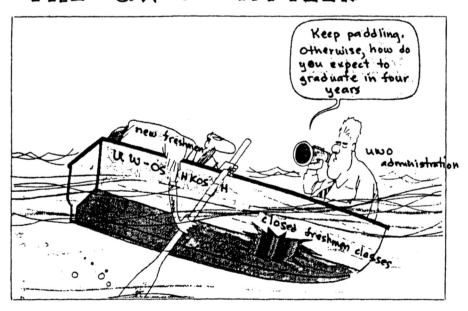

in the next episode. Dean will always be remembered, especially at Christmas time.

December 1st is National AIDS Awareness Day. Some years we attend one of the observances in the Tampa Area. We have been to programs at both the Hospice of Tampa and at St. Joseph Hospital.

Once the Dean book was published we joined the AIDS/Health subcommittee of the Church and Society Committee of the Presbytery of Tampa Bay. Through this committee we helped co-ordinate AIDS awareness activities by providing materials to the 78 Presbyterian churches in our area. AIDS programs for the congregation were made available.

Newspaper articles in local newspapers provided me with several opportunities to speak to the Men's Fellowship of area churches.

Finally, a web site was set up to make the book available nationally and to link up with other AIDS sites.

Restored Mental Health With: A Father's Story

An early death for Dean certainly wasn't our plan. But it happened, we had to deal with it, resolve issues in our minds and, somehow, move on. It's the moving on which is difficult. Getting over that hump which is likened to a speed bump on the road of life.

Writing became my psychotherapy to get me over the hump. By mid 1997 this was accomplished and I wrote about that feat in a story published in June of 2000. This is the article, with only the first few sentences eliminated to avoid repetition, as it appeared in, Chicken Soup for the Writer's Soul.

Dean Has AIDS—A Father's Story

It was one of those lazy Sunday afternoons and I was watching professional football. My wife decided to call our third son, now living two thousand miles away, to clarify a comment he made in his last letter.

I became aware of my wife's silence as she sat motionless on the floor holding the phone. "Honey, what's wrong?" I asked. Slowly she looked up. Finally she said, "AIDS—Dean has AIDS". The ordeal lasted twenty-one months with our son moving in

with us for the final fifteen. Care giving our son saw us experience nine life and death situations, rejected by our church and shunned by many friends. AIDS will do that.

Help started coming after the local newspaper began running a series on AIDS featuring Dean, my wife and me, and our trials for community education and awareness.

Dean died May 23, 1993. In the aftermath my wife had a frozen shoulder and was an emotional wreck. She knew immediately the price paid physically and mentally.

Six months later I lay on a hospital bed with doctors advising me to retire immediately, that my immune system had crashed and psoriatic arthritis had immobilized my joints. All as a result of the stress just experienced.

How does a man grieve and release pent-up emotions? Women seem to be able to ventilate to friends and talk out feelings. But us men?....we spend our time talking about: athletics, hunting or fishing, our job, hobbies, politics or the "the old days".

I began to write. First certain episodes, then listing all that had happened to us. I expanded on areas that represented our greatest hurt. I needed answers to questions relating to why people acted the way they did. I knew I would remain emotionally sick unless I could begin forgiving. But I had to identify what had to be forgiven. On paper I identified all options and reasoned why certain options were chosen: More organizing, more outlining, more fleshing out the outline entries.

Soon I had a hand written manuscript. A former secretary typed the manuscript on her computer and the editor of the newspaper which ran our story did the editing.

Fifty publishers were contacted, seventeen read the manuscript and one requested a ninety day exclusive option. I talked to several editors. All agreed the quality of the writing was good, the story neatly developed and that its message should be made available to the public but "...we're a business. Unless you are a known individual like, O. J. Simpson, the public won't buy a biographical story – even when the subject is AIDS. My list of books for publication will be approved only if I can convince my review committee that the projected profit on your book is higher that another candidate."

On the recommendation of a friend I contracted with a publisher to self-publish my book.

My book arrived two years ago. To contact my anticipated audience I wrote to every hospice, infectious disease physician and community based AIDS support service in the country and offered the book through direct mail. Then through two distributors and the internet, I offered the book to the general public.

Having published my book gave me instant acceptance as an expert on the social impact of AIDS. Newspaper articles resulted in opportunities to give talks in churches. The distributors opened doors for talks and signings at bookstores.

I now realize that having published my book gave me an opportunity to first write out my feelings and then talk them out while providing emotional support to those affected by AIDS or any other disease which takes life prematurely. I began to feel my head emptied of that which could have destroyed me emotionally. I have now grieved my loss and my life is back together again.

We are now able to move on with life. Having a new found skill in writing is helping me to feel like a "Grandma Moses" – but writing, not painting. Funny, I barely passed English in college and never considered myself a writer. Now a second manuscript is almost done and a third book is in the thinking stage. My lemons have become lemonade.

Edmund Hansen

Mother's Death

It was 9:45 AM Saturday January 6, 1996. I looked around the chapel in Highland Memorial Park. Mother's casket was closed with an 8 by 10 inch portrait on top. She was smiling in the picture, taken in better days before her illness. Ginny and my brother, Jim, were sitting next to me.

Also next to the casket was a wreath held in place by a stand. Made of woven grape vines it contained magnolia flowers and other greens plus an angel in the center. Paul Panske and his brother, Tony, made the wreath and provided the flowers

Paul and his friend, Karen Paulik, would sing "Be not Afraid" and "How Great Thou Art" during the service.

slowly, I held up my hand with its palm facing Ginny. She was watching me and stopped in her tracks. Slowly, slowly, slowly I lowered my index finger pointing to them. Soon she broke into a big smile of recognition. We had a big laugh together as we realized that we had set our chairs in the middle of a community of sand crabs, who were more afraid of us than we of them. We watched them for another hour or so, took our chairs back to the van and called it a day. A day for our memory bank of Florida experiences.

Exotic Cruises, Elderhostels and What Else I do with My Time

"Tell me Ed, why do you want to cruise the Baltic Sea?" Everyone was asking this question whenever I told them about this trip. The answer, to me, was obvious,

"You know, I'm Danish. In the ninth century my forefathers, the furious and feared Vikings, sailed the Baltic Sea in their long boats. It seems only respectful to them that I visit the lands they raped and pillaged."

The United Community Church of Sun City Center sponsors what they call the Community College. Residents with expertise in certain areas offer classes for fellow residents.

One class I took was in Irish history. Talking about the ninth century and the Viking invasions the teacher said,

"They were thugs, just plain thugs."

I proceeded to introduce myself during coffee break as,

"A man sired by thugs."

To see the land my uncles and aunts talked about has always been a dream of mine. In 1997 we decided to act on that dream and

I am Hansen-The-Horrible. My great-great-.....great forefathers roamed the seas in their long boats exploring and raping and pillaging. We are a feared people.

signed up for a cruise upon the Baltic Sea.

The cruise itinerary including embarkation from Dover, England with ports of call: Amsterdam, Netherlands; Copenhagen, Denmark; Stockholm, Sweden; Helsinki, Finland; St. Petersburg, Russia; Tallinn, Estonia; Riga, Latvia; Gdynia, Poland (the port for Gdansk); and a trip through the Kiel Canal connecting the Baltic Sea to the North Sea enroute back to Dover. We added an "early bird" onto the cruise and spent three days touring England.

With my limited mobility I confined my shore excursions to bus or canal trips, with the exception of a tour of the Czar's summer home, the Peterhof Palace and the Hermitage museum in St. Petersburg. The latter contains the world's greatest collection of paintings.

Seeing the Scandinavian countries and the Baltic countries exceeded my expectations. One of the unforgettable experiences was seeing the opulence of the Netherlands, Denmark, Sweden and Finland and then to compare this to the depressed former Soviet bloc countries of Russia, Estonia, Latvia and Poland. Seeing nothing but poorly built apartment buildings and having no single family homes built since before WWII in the Soviet countries was very depressing.

The Estonian tour guide said that the average family income was around $280 per month and retired couples receive a pension of $80 per month. Private ownership of automobiles—preowned of course and from the West—was just starting.

The Russian tour guide had already given up her small business ownership dream, first permitted starting in 1990, because crime and protection money prevented her from succeeding.

The tour buses in the East were pathetic. These buses would be on the junk heap in the USA.

We returned with a real appreciation of what we have in the USA. A feeling of being very wealthy. I appreciated especially the handicapped facilities in the USA since I saw none, absolutely none, in the former Soviet bloc countries.

Our second exotic cruise was down the Amazon River. Why the Amazon River you ask? To see the river and what the rain forest is like.

The Amazon River is the second longest river in the world with

a length of 4100 miles. While the Nile River is 100 miles longer, the volume of water flowing in the Amazon is 200 times greater. Its length is Compare this to the Mississippi River in the USA. Its length is 2,350 miles long.

The Mississippi River has been banked with levees, spanned with bridges for cars and trains, dredged for shipping and has locks installed in certain areas to facilitate movement of ships. I wanted to see a major river not yet adulterated nor contained by man.

We flew the 2500 miles from Miami to Manaus, Brazil on a charter flight. There we boarded the Royal Princess along with 1200 other passengers. The 756-foot, nine-deck cruise ship with a crew of 600 was ready for us with an exciting eleven-day trip.

It was the day before Carnival when we boarded. Like Mardi Gras in New Orleans, Carnival has a religious origin and in South America is celebrated with carnivals and parades whose participants are high costumed. These costumes usually involve feathered headdresses several yards wide. Except for boots, the rest of them are x-rated. We were entertained with a show on board the ship and really enjoyed the extravagance of it.

The Amazon River is fully navigable the 1000 miles up to Manaus. The city, about two million in population, assembles electronics which are hauled by ship to Manaus and, when assembled, shipped back down the river. Only two roads leave Manaus with one dead-ending in the rain forest after 200 miles. All transportation to and from Manaus is done by boat.

The poverty in Manaus, like other third world cities, is

Here we are on our very first cruise. These exotic parrots always fascinated me. This cruise, in the fall of 1994, went to the Western Caribbean.

unbelievable unless you see it with our own eyes.

The cruise headed down the Amazon River with two more Brazilian ports-of-call. Once in the South Atlantic we turned north with stops at: Devil's Island, French Guinea; Trinidad; La Guaira, Venezuela (where we were bused to its' capitol, Caracas); Curacao, Netherlands Antilles; and ending in San Juan, Puerto Rico.

We have also taken three domestic cruises including the Western and Eastern Caribbean plus Bermuda.

To date we have participated in five Elderhostels to Statesboro, Georgia; New Orleans, Louisiana; Haynesville, North Carolina; and two in Florida at St. Augustine and Key West. These educational experiences are terrific. And the people we met have been fabulous.

The retirement community of Sun City Center, a city of around fifteen thousand, has recreation centers, classes, 126 holes of golf, tennis courts, English lawn bowling, touring professional entertainment and many swimming pools. One of the satellite pools is very near our condo and this is where we do our "swimming."

Our fourth cruise was in Spring of 1998 and took us to Bermuda. We found cruising so enjoyable that I purchased my own white dinner jacket. I hadn't owned one of those since my prom days in high school. For some of our entertainment we would allow ourselves $20 per day for the slot machines. The third day out Ginny won the jack pot for $1250.

We really don't swim. Residents tend to show up at the same time every day. Once a time slot is chosen fellow swimmers become well known to each other. Most of us stand around in the water, "steeping", fraternizing and solving the world's problems. Just ask us. We have the answers to all the world's problems.

During our first three years here in Sun City Center we purchased annual passes to both Disney World and Busch Gardens/Sea world. Once or twice a month we were off to a theme park. After three years we were beginning to see Mickey Mouse in our sleep. It was time for a change.

Our interest transferred to watching Broadway productions at the Tampa Bay Performing Arts Center. We obtained a season pass good for seven performances each year. In addition, we began attending performances at the Florida Symphony Orchestra. This became very culturally enriching for us.

Do I have a hobby? Yes, I have a hobby. I love to write. Almost anything non-fiction interests me. My credits include, besides publishing the Dean book, four articles in the Tampa Tribune with several appearing in this book, plus a short story in <u>Chicken Soup for the Writer's Soul</u>.

I was simply thrilled when notified of the acceptance of the Chicken Soup story. Believe me to have my writings appear with those of Steve Allen, Dave Barry and Agatha Christie have put me on a life-time high.

Do I now regret being forced into a premature retirement? Absolutely not. Ginny and I are having the time of our lives. Really quality time together without life's' distractions. These have become 'The Golden Years'; the last for which the first were made.

Key West Replaces Door County

Before my retirement one of our favorite destinations for rest and recuperation was Door County (DC), that little finger like peninsula protruding into Lake Michigan just above Green Bay.

I remember going to DC as a kid with my parents to Peninsula State Park for picnics, especially in the fall during color season. Ginny and I would camp in the park three weeks each summer with our "love nest" camper. This was when our sons were already launched. After we moved to the condo and sold the camper

Everyone is not only out of high school but we are one day before the last wedding. The date is December 22, 1987. L - R back row is Kelley, Perry, Julia, Lee and Scott; front row Dean, me, Ginny, Robin and Eric. Eric is 6 months old.

EPILOGUE

Ginny is typing these memoirs. Family difficulties, obligations and responsibilities have slowed her pace. June, Ginny's mother, was diagnosed with Alzheimer's disease in late spring of 2000. Bert, her stepfather, has experienced several mini strokes. Both were moved to assisted living in Green Bay, Wisconsin during July. While both of us are in our 60's we are still in the sandwich generation category.

On the lighter side, Melanie traveled to Florida to spend a week with us in June. Melanie had reached the magic age of eight. It was a fun time for all. And these visits by loved ones are more precious than diamonds.

P. S. from Ginny, I finished the first draft of typing on April 1, 2001. I thought it would be fun to say, "I'm finished, 'April fool'." Ed had his doubts I'd finish this. Plus it's only right that since I'm doing the typing that I have the "last word." (But we're not competitive!)

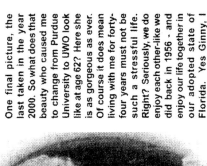

One final picture, the last taken in the year 2000. So what does that beauty who caused me to change from Purdue University to UWO look like at age 62? Here she is as gorgeous as ever. Of course it does mean living with me for forty-four years must not be such a stressful life. Right? Seriously, we do enjoy each other-like we did back in 1956 - and enjoy our life together in our adopted state of Florida. Yes Ginny, I love you very much.

398

176

Fairway Press is pleased to announce the publication of...

A FATHER'S STORY

The Story of a Son's Battle with AIDS

By Edmund Hansen

A FATHER'S STORY is a true story profiling the author's personal struggle in coping with the suffering and eventual loss of an AIDS victim — his son. This heart-warming and inspiring book, written from a Judeo-Christian perspective, confronts the issues of AIDS, homosexuality and its impact on family living.

A Father's Story
The Story of a Son's Battle with AIDS
Edmund Hansen with Jo Zorr

ISBN 0-7880-0663 $9.95

"I think this book is right down to where the rubber meets the road to help reveal the hurt and pain families endure when faced with caring for an AIDS patient. It is warm, loving and will provide insights for those on the outside looking in."

Barbara Johnson
Author, *Stick a Geranium in Your Hat and Be Happy*
Founder of Spatula Ministries

Edmund Hansen and his wife reside in Sun City Center, Florida. Mr. Hansen was compelled to publish his book to provide people with a firsthand understanding of the effects that such a loss has on an AIDS victim's family; an understanding he believed needed to be explored as the interest in this country in AIDS-related issues continues to grow.

Please send me _____ copies of *A FATHER'S STORY: The Story of a Son's Battle with AIDS* (Book #663-0). Enclosed please find $9.95 per copy plus tax, postage and handling.

ORDER BLANK

Quantity	Item Number	Price
	Florida Residents add 6.5% sales tax	
	subtotal	
	shipping & handling	
	TOTAL	

Name _____

Street Address _____

City _____ State _____ Zip _____

Phone _____

A.   When ordering from the author, please send check or money order to:

Edmund R. Hansen
1011 Norfork Island Court
Sun City Center, FL 33573

Please add proper shipping, tax and handling:

| 1-3 copies | add $2.75 | 8-11 copies | add $4.00 |
| 4-7 copies | add $3.50 | 12 and over | add $4.75 |

Hans Hagar Press is pleased to announce the publication of:

FROM GRANDSON TO GRANDFATHER

Reflections of a University Professor on His Career and Family

Key Topics in this book about Edmund Hansen

1. His peaks and valleys experienced living life.

2. The changing life 'hats' from son and grandson, giving way to husband and father and, finally, grandfather.

3. His role as sweetheart, lover and husband to the same woman for forty-five years (as of 2001).

4. The antidotal humorous stories told about raising four sons.

5. His insightful perspective as a faculty member living through forty years of the history of the University of Wisconsin - Oshkosh as it went from a teachers college of 500 students to a regional university encompassing four undergraduate colleges with 12,000 students.

6. His candid portrayal of the individuals employed at the university in key positions as the school went through the civil rights riots of the 60's, the financial crises which precipitated the tremendous changes of the 70's, and its emergence as a school of academic excellence, i.e., its Golden Age, in the 80's.

Key Writing Features in this book by Edmund Hansen

1. Family stories are told in episode format. An episode, like family camping, is told in its entirety and not integrated piece-meal chronologically with other on-going activities.

2. Career periods are told intact in separate chapters and not integrated with family activities. This allows the reader to separate the family man from the university professor.

ISBN 0-9709434-0-7

$14.95

ORDER FORM:

Please send me _____ copies of From Grandson to Grandfather at $14.95 each plus shipping and handling.

To order send to: Edmund Hansen, 1011 Norfolk Island Court, Sun City Center, FL 33573

Name _____

Address _____

City _____ State _____ Zip _____

Phone (_____) _____

Shipping: Please add $4.00 for the first book and $1.00 for each additional book shipped to the same address.

Make check payable to EDMUND HANSEN

ABOUT THE AUTHOR

Edmund Hansen graduated with a B.S. degree from the University of Wisconsin—Oshkosh and an M.S. degree from the University of Kansas. In addition he had extensive postgraduate training at Tulane University and the University of Kansas.

Edmund taught for 3 years in secondary schools and 31 years at his alma mater, the University of Wisconsin—Oshkosh. His university career was split between the teaching of mathematics and administration, ending his collegiate career as the Coordinator of Academic Advisement for the College of Business Administration. As a university administrator Edmund frequently wrote technical reports and position papers.

Following an early retirement Edmund turned his attention to personal writing. After he and his wife completed care giving their third son he penned the book, A Father's Story: The Story of a Son's Battle with AIDS.

This book was followed by a 406-page memoir, From Grandson to Grandfather: Reflections of a University Professor on his Career and Family. His wife's memoirs were next and he wrote, Grin and Share It: The Story of a Loyal Daughter's Quest for a Meaningful Relationship with Her Mother.

In addition to three published books Edmund has written many short stories for "The Tampa Tribune" in the 'I Remember It Well' section. He has written for the "Lutheran" magazine and has a short story in Chicken Soup for the Writer's Soul. This latter short story related his search for a publisher of his first book and how the writing of this book was his method of grieving the death of his son.

Mr. Hansen has taught a course entitled 'Writing Your Memoirs' at a local community college for the last three years. It is from this experience that he wrote his fourth book. How to Write Slices of Life: The Episode Approach to Memoir Writing

Printed in the United States
39517LVS00002B/313